Southern Foodways and Culture

Southern Foodways and Culture: Local Considerations and Beyond

Edited by
Lisa J. Lefler

Selected Papers from the Annual Meeting of the
Southern Anthropological Society,
Oxford, Mississippi
February, 2007

Robert Shanafelt, Series Editor

Newfound Press
THE UNIVERSITY OF TENNESSEE LIBRARIES, KNOXVILLE

Southern Anthropological Society
Founded 1966

Southern Foodways and Culture: Local Considerations and Beyond
© 2013 by Southern Anthropological Society: http://southernanthro.org/

Digital version at www.newfoundpress.utk.edu/pubs/foodways
Print on demand available through University of Tennessee Press.

Newfound Press is a digital imprint of the University of Tennessee Libraries. Its publications are available for non-commercial and educational uses, such as research, teaching and private study. The author has licensed the work under the Creative Commons Attribution-Noncommercial 3.0 United States License. To view a copy of this license, visit http://creativecommons.org/licenses/by-nc/3.0/us/

For all other uses, contact:

Newfound Press
University of Tennessee Libraries
1015 Volunteer Boulevard
Knoxville, TN 37996-1000
www.newfoundpress.utk.edu

ISBN-13: 978-0-9846445-4-4
ISBN-10: 0-9846445-4-7

Southern foodways and culture / edited by Lisa J. Lefler ; Robert Shanafelt, series editor.
Knoxville, Tenn : Newfound Press, University of Tennessee Libraries, c2013.
1 online resource (x, 188 p.)
Includes bibliographical references.
1. Cooking, American -- Southern style -- Social aspects -- Congresses. 2. Food -- Social aspects -- Southern States -- Congresses. 3. Southern States -- Social life and customs -- Congresses. I. Lefler, Lisa J.
II. Southern Anthropological Society. Meeting.
TX715.2.S68 S644 2013

Book design by Jayne W. Smith
Cover design by Stephanie Thompson

Contents

Introduction   1
Lisa J. Lefler

Ramps: Appalachian Delicacies that "Smells God-Awful, but Cures what Ails Ya"   7
Lisa J. Lefler

The Politics of Traditional Foodways in the Arkansas Delta   19
C. Laine Gates, Justin M. Nolan, and Mary Jo Schneider

Cherokee Snakebite Remedies   43
David Cozzo

Fair Fare?: Food as Contested Terrain in US Prisons and Jails   67
Avi Brisman

Teaching Anthropology Through Food   147
David M. Johnson

Contributors   181

Introduction

Lisa J. Lefler

We all are consumers of the planet. One of the cultural universals that provides anthropologists with ample opportunity for trepidation, joy, and curiosity is eating. This volume represents the work of anthropologists who share interest in the importance of food and in the use of plants and animals. During the forty-sixth annual meeting of the Southern Anthropological Society, held in Oxford, Mississippi, we had the pleasure of meeting at the Mecca of Southern food enthusiasts, chefs, and food documentarians—the University of Mississippi. Our discussions and papers about plants and food represent common activities at Ole Miss, as this is the home of the Southern Foodways Alliance. This organization, housed at the University's Center for the Study of Southern Culture, provides the perfect backdrop for foodways themes. By their own definition, the Southern Foodways Alliance "documents, studies, and celebrates the diverse food cultures of the changing American South" (http://www.southernfoodways.org/). Southern food and Southern cooking have long been popular genres for cookbooks, cooking shows, and magazines. For many years, for example, *Southern Living* magazine has provided interested hosts and hostesses, living both north and south of the Mason Dixon line, with recipes and dining suggestions. *Garden & Gun*, a relatively new magazine in this genre, combines two mainstays of Southern culture, providing readers with tips about food, as well as covering stories for enthusiasts of producing and hunting it for themselves.

Anthropologists are also interested in what people eat, where people eat, why people eat the things they do, and what food may represent to them. We want to know about the meaning and context of food—how it is gathered, how it is processed, what it means to the gatherers and tenders of the soil—and to understand multiple uses of plants as food and medicine and how food contributes uniquely to identity.

Cultural considerations of food and foodways include the way people perceive the place and role of certain foods. For example, among the Eastern Cherokee, a spring green called *sochan* not only is a nutritious plant that provides important vitamins to the diet, but it is also a meaningful thing that provides a unique connection for the Cherokee people. Not many people who live outside the homeland of the Eastern Band of Cherokee Indians have ever heard of sochan. For those in the know, however, this plant is highly celebrated. It can be commonly found at large family gatherings and homecomings. Even the physical activities that surround the gathering of the plants in the Great Smoky Mountains Region of Western North Carolina are valued memories among the Cherokees. Other people often do not understand. Recently, several members of a Cherokee family appeared in federal court for gathering sochan in the nearby national park. At the hearing, traditionalists from the tribe who testified before the federal judge pointed out that this plant is of extreme importance to their people and that the annual gathering in that place had been done for thousands of years.

Sochan is an important spring staple that provides nutrition, but the Cherokee also believe in the plant's medicinal properties, for instance, in its value for "cleaning the blood." Like ramps, another regional delicacy addressed in this volume, gathering sochan is perceived as a family tradition and spring ritual that provides an opportunity for physical activity and for creating memories of time spent together with children, parents, and grandparents. Sochan can also represent a place of harvest that has been identified by one's ancestors and kept a family secret for generations. Furthermore, these generationally kept, secret locations can be sources of great sadness, as many of them are now inaccessible. Economic development of the land, which actually results in destruction of the land and its flora and fauna, or new ownership of the land, which often includes "no trespassing" signs and fences, both restrict access to patches of edible and medicinal plants and prohibit the socializing that is synonymous with the annual seasonal family outings to gather traditional foods.

Southern foods help identify various regions, ethnicities, histories, and ecosystems. They are the substance of memories of fishing, hunting, planting, gathering, harvesting, "putting up," and of family gatherings where foods were prepared and consumed. Even the vessels in which foods were cooked are artifacts of culture and place. Cast iron cookware is pretty much a Southern universal. "Gritters" (punched tins attached to wooden boards to coarsely rip dried kernels of corn for meal), butter churns, crock jars, cabbage cutters, and yes, "stills" were all representative of region, class, and ethnicity. Blacksmiths, potters, woodworkers, and other regional artisans all contributed to the preparation of Southern food.

A great understanding of regional ecosystems often was associated with the harvesting and preparation of food. Mountain subsistence farmers often planted by the "signs" and took a great deal of caution when deciding to break ground, when to plant tubers, and when to sow those vegetables that would bear fruit topside of the soil. As part of preserving the rapidly changing lifeways of mountain living, high school students in Rabun County, Georgia, collected local stories of planting by the signs, Appalachian cookery, and

Appalachian winemaking, which are included in various books for the now famous *Foxfire* collection.

Other local color publications come in the form of regional cookbooks. From the Delta to the Atlantic coast, one can find church and civic groups who have gathered family-favorite recipes and printed them for fundraisers. In many of these cookbooks, stories about why certain foods or dishes were popular to the region are explained in short paragraphs and provide "outsiders" with a glimpse into the food world of that community. For some people, these cookbooks are like sacred texts in that they have included handwritten recipes from relatives and experiences of years past. They hold not only recipes that satisfy physical hunger but also provide keepsakes of emotional attachments. When these family cookbooks are lost or damaged, lasting sadness is associated with those handwritten notes and quirky ingredients that old friends and relatives shared.

Not only do foods such as barbecue, grits, and cracklins hold a place in the hearts of Southerners, so do their drinks. While living and doing research in Oklahoma, I heard conflicting discussion on the placement of the state: Is Oklahoma a Southern state or a Midwestern state? It wasn't hard for me to weigh in, as I quickly found that 90 percent of the restaurants in which I ordered tea did not put sugar in the boil as they prepared it. Sweetened iced tea, "sweet tea," is a staple of Southern living, and a state that doesn't offer this drink as a regular menu item could never be considered a Southern state. Other drinks (besides corn "likker," of course), that are of Southern heritage include mint juleps, buttermilk, and a host of sodas or soft drinks. Coca Cola and Pepsi originated in the South, and several regions claim fame to other brands such as Cheerwine (North Carolina), "Blenheim Ginger Ale (South Carolina), Buffalo Rock Ale (Alabama), Pop Rouge (Louisiana), Dr. Enuf (Tennessee), and Ale 81 (Kentucky)" (Egerton 1987).

Southerners are also known for their "sweet tooth," and a meal is never complete without dessert. Seasonal fruit cobblers, made primarily from berries that can be gathered in rural fields, included gooseberries, blueberries, blackberries, raspberries, huckleberries, wild strawberries, and mulberries. These berries would be picked as they came abundant during various seasons of the year. Shoo Fly pie, divinity, stack cakes, fried apple pies, congealed fruit salads, and chess pies are all desserts that provide guests an opportunity to make primal noises denoting approval to their Southern host.

People of the South speak of food as often and casually as others talk about the weather. We speak of special dishes, local diners, and annual food-centered events. We talk about what we ate when we were growing up, how food was prepared, and how it tasted. Inevitably, memories emerge of grandmothers in the kitchen: at a woodstove making biscuits and gravy, next to a large iron cauldron making hominy, putting up jars of "bleached fruit," or preparing enough food for dozens of family members and guests for a holiday meal. Each memory is so vivid you can smell it.

As we think of Southern foodways and celebrate how food represents diversity in the South and characterizes the South, this volume offers perspectives that perhaps would not be addressed in a general volume on Southern food. To be sure, their ethnographic focus is primarily centered on the South. The chapter, by volume editor Lisa Lefler, discusses ramps—a leek-like wild bulb—and its place in her Appalachian family and culture; the chapter by C. Laine Gates, Justin M. Nolan, and Mary Jo Schneider discusses political issues relating to obesity in the Arkansas Delta; and the chapter by ethnobotanist David Cozzo explains what Cherokees of the region believe about medicinal plants native to the region and how they use them—specifically with reference to snakebites. But our considerations, if they ever really could be, are not exclusively confined to some "pure"

Southern realm. Rather, consideration of the local also raises questions about links elsewhere. The study of food also provides a venue for the analysis of other things, including relationships of power. In addition to the political issues raised by Gates, Nolan, and Schneider, Avi Brisman's work also turns our attention to issues of political control in relationship to food, focusing on how food service operates in prisons. This erudite article, presented initially for SAS, subsequently modified for publication in the journal *Georgetown Journal on Poverty Law and Policy*,[1] considers food in prisons from a wide range of cross-cultural settings. Similarly, David Johnson considers food more generally, and he discusses how issues relating to food can be used in anthropology courses to teach students about culture. David Cozzo's analysis of ethnobotany has similarly wide potential for application.

Clearly, food satisfies hunger, but it can help us understand other things as well. It is prepared as part of a daily routine, but it also may be sacred. It is wound up with history, culture, and place, and also who makes, monitors, and controls it. Southerners know that food—particularly as it is paired with music—is as unifying as spiritual enlightenment and as euphoric as sex. It is a topic of limitless possibilities; and for many anthropologists, a topic not just to be studied but to be sampled and enjoyed.

Note

1. In volume 15, issue 49.

Work Cited

Egerton, John. 1987. *Southern Food: At Home, On the Road, and in History*. Chapel Hill: University of North Carolina Press.

Ramps: Appalachian Delicacies that "Smells God-Awful, but Cures what Ails Ya"

Lisa J. Lefler

Michael Ann Williams' wonderful book *Great Smoky Mountains Folklife* skillfully describes how important foodways[1] are in defining Smoky Mountain culture. Acknowledging the many changes that fast food and modernization have brought to the area in the last three decades, she still speaks to "meanings attached to specific foods and customs that surround them." She also relays a multitude of stories from families' memories of food grown, harvested, cooked, prepared, preserved, and shared. She says that "food still plays an important role in defining the past" (1995). And like people that I spoke with from Cherokee, North Carolina, and surrounding communities, many of the most inspired stories came from those about harvesting wild foods, particularly ramps. Foods were seasonal and generated memories that were associated with specific times of the year and with other events that made "putting up" and sharing foods important. This seasonal gathering was entangled with family and community identity and was part of being a mountain person or Indian.

Family Recollections about Ramps

As a young girl growing up in Western North Carolina, every spring, my father and I always excitedly anticipated one of the greatest gifts the mountains had to offer—ramps. This plant, a relative to wild leeks, was the quest of our annual trek high up a steeply sloping mountain ravine whose location was a closely guarded family secret. However, in recent years, after my father had lost his leg and eyesight to diabetes, he shared his secret locations with those who would accompany him to gather these luscious delicacies. He would park his wheelchair at the top of the ravine where he could look down in our general vicinity and shout directions about where we should be looking and digging.

When our burlap sacks had been filled completely, we brought them home, washed them and cut off the long, green, lily-like tops outside the house, so as not to smell things up inside. We then brought the small but flavor-packed bulbs to mom so she could cut some of them up for a meal that day and put the rest up for our use the rest of the year. Some she would parboil and tightly wrap to put in the refrigerator for immediate consumption, but most she would freeze. In years past, dad would have them scrambled with eggs or squirrel brains, but the most preferred meal for our family was fried potatoes with ramps, along with fresh mountain trout. Sometimes we would invite friends and neighbors over and have a major fish fry complete with hushpuppies and coleslaw. After a long winter of potatoes, canned beans, and soup, ramps provided a tasty change, not to mention the tonic-like benefits mom told us they provided. Like onions, "they're good for your heart," she'd say.

I asked mom about the first time she'd ever eaten ramps, and she said her grandmother, Alma, had brought them over from high up Connelly's Creek and introduced them to her dad's family, and they began to grow them in a small patch above the fields. Interestingly though, she didn't remember eating them until after she was married, at about nineteen years of age. She said her paternal Grandma Alma was of Cherokee descent, and her folks from Connelly's Creek ate them, but neither her mother nor maternal grandmother ever ate or talked about ramps.

I found this curious since ramps have long been harvested by the Cherokees, and white settlers knew about them not long after contact. Rattray (2003) states, "The word [*ramp*] is first mentioned in English print in 1530 but was used earlier by English immigrants of the Southern Appalachian Mountains." Like my mother's experience, even some Cherokees didn't try ramps until they were young adults; specifically, those who didn't grow up in Western North Carolina. One forty-six-year-old Cherokee woman remembers being introduced to ramps when she was a young adult. She was a self-identified "Airforce brat" and had come back to Cherokee to live with her mother and matrilineal family when she was in her late teens. When asked about her experience with ramps, she was quick to tell me she had eaten ramps regularly for the past thirty years but remembers her first encounter with the "little, slimy, green wild plants." She said when her family introduced her to them, she wasn't about to eat those smelly things, but soon she became acquainted with their unusual flavor and was told of their medicinal properties. She said, "They smell god-awful, but they cure what ails ya." Now she eats them and looks forward to their arrival every year in the very early spring.

She said the best way to prepare them is to parboil them and chop them up, and fry them with eggs or potatoes. To freeze them, just clean them really good and make sure they're dry before "puttin' 'em up." Another Cherokee female, aged 28, relayed that her father had planted a ramp patch up the mountain behind their home. "He never would let anyone else in the patch, and since he died," she said, "my brother is the only one allowed to go." She remembered the ritual of having fresh ramps in the early spring, sometimes along with branch lettuce. She said, "My mom would cut up a bowl of ramps, and then fix a bowl of branch lettuce, slice boiled eggs, and layer them on top of it with fried bacon—so crisp it was almost black, and then mom would pour the hot bacon grease on top to kill it. That was a great meal."

In recent conversations with these women, just before presenting this paper at a Southern Anthropological Society conference, both mentioned that they had uncles who had already gone in early January to dig for ramps. They said the ramps were very young and green but still ready for digging. An unusually warm winter was cited as instigating the early harvest. Historically, Cherokees harvested ramps earlier than their white neighbors and ate the pungent tiny bulbs along with most of the green leaves. White families often waited till closer to Easter and usually didn't eat too far up the green stalk.

Others with whom I spoke about harvesting ramps generally spoke fondly, even longingly, of years past and their fathers and uncles would take them to the ramp patch. One man, about sixty years of age, smiled and recounted the springtimes of his youth when his uncle would take him well up on the mountain to gather ramps:

> We'd go way up Nantahala to a place that spread out wide between the ridges. I remember so clearly a stand of white oaks, and the ground was so dark and rich and soft, you could just reach down under those oaks and pull up a bunch of ramps, and then shake 'em real good, and the dirt would just fall off of 'em clean. You didn't even have to wash 'em, you could eat 'em right then and there. That was the most beautiful place in the spring. The ramps would grow in one long field, and the wind would blow, and those big broad green leaves would just sway in waves. Sometimes we'd just get enough to cook that evening after going trout fishing, and my uncle

would cook it all up right there on the creek bank. Now that was good eatin'. Those were wonderful times.

I asked him if they ever "put up" or canned ramps, and he said, "Law, yea. We put up just about everything we grew or harvested, but there were also a lot of things we pickled. Mom pickled okra, beans, corn, beets, and ramps, just to name a few." There were also stories about eating ramps so that you wouldn't have to go to school. One man in his late fifties recounted a boy in his class who spent most of the early spring listening to their teacher from the hallway. "Yea, there were some who knew they wouldn't have to go to class if they ate raw ramps. You could smell 'em a mile."

Ramps as Medicine

One of the consistent themes referred to in these conversations is the medicinal properties of ramps. Most mentioned that ramps cleansed or strengthened the blood, while others would just say it was a spring tonic. The historic record shows that some Native peoples used them to treat bee stings and coughs and colds, specifically citing the Menomini who referred to ramps as *skunk plants*. The reference to a now famous city on Lake Michigan reflects this place originally as skunk place, or CicagaWuni [Chicago], a place where ramps are many (Birringer et al. 2002).

Four decades ago, the research of Zennie and Ogzewalla (1974) stated that ramps "compared with oranges, on a weight basis, had higher values of vitamin C." Other studies have shown that ramps or *Alliums* are a good source of vitamin C and "prostaglandin A1—a fatty acid known to be therapeutic in the treatment of hypertension" (2002). Birringer et al. say that "studies have linked the genus to increases in the production of high-density lipoproteins, which in turn are believed to combat heart disease by reducing blood serum levels of cholesterol."

A 2000 article by Whanger et al. stated that ramps (*Allium tricoccum*) contain selenium and concluded that "selenium-enriched ramps appear to have potential for the reduction of cancer in humans" (5723). In addition, it's thought that the "allicin (diallysulfide oxide) in ramps, which has antibiotic properties, has also been linked to reduced rates of cancer (Block 2005).

In other research, ramps have been found to "contain cepaenes, which function as antithrombotic agents," (Calvey et al. 1998) and "flavonoids, and other antioxidants that are free-radical scavengers" (Crellin and Philpott 1990). As often happens, cultural beliefs about the healing qualities of wild plants, in this case—ramps—prove to bear true in scientific analyses.

Where are They?

A 1979 article by botanist Almut Jones shows that ramps can be found from the far-northeastern United States, just north of Maine, down the Appalachian Mountains, into northern Alabama and Georgia, across the northern Midwest, throughout the Great Lakes region, from Wisconsin, back down to Iowa. He identifies two varieties of ramps—*Allium tricoccum* and *Allium burdickii*, the former being "conspicuously larger," with a difference in pigment and flowering (30). The distribution for A. burdickii is similar to A. tricoccum; however, Jones shows far fewer findings of A. burdickii along the Eastern Mountain ranges. A team of Forest Service botanists, led by Gary Kauffman (2001), conducted ramp research in the Southern Appalachian region in 2001 and found that "there is no consistent evidence available to verify the presence of A. burdickii in North Carolina as a species morphologically distinct from A. tricoccum." A. tricoccum is considered to be the plant that was much earlier identified in writings about wild leeks and was introduced into English gardens by 1770 (Jones 1979, 30). A. burdickii was identified in 1877 in Wisconsin and became the namesake of the naturalist who wrote about it—J. H. Burdick.

Only one person interviewed from Cherokee mentioned that there might be two different plants, only one of which they harvested for consumption. He said, "like most plants put here for us, there is a copy-cat plant that we shouldn't use and one that we should." In my past conversations with folks about medicinal plants in general, the consensus is that plants will "show themselves to those who know how to use them." Cherokee elders Jerry Wolfe and Walker Calhoun have spoken about going out to harvest plants, and the "right" plant showing itself by shaking. They credit this also as a way to conserve these very precious, yet threatened, plants. On a locally made commercial video about Cherokee plants, Mr. Wolfe shows the proper way to harvest a ramp plant. He pulls up the plant until the bulb comes almost out of the ground, and then slices off the bulb at the root, allowing the root to remain protected in the ground. He says that most people just come in and pull them up without considering how not leaving the root will detrimentally impact future ramp harvests.

Overharvesting and improper harvesting have resulted in dramatic population decline of mountain ramps. A recent Forest Service report also indicated that changes in weather and elevation can also affect ramp abundance (Walker, Silletti, and White 2005). Ramps are usually found at elevations between 3500 ft. and just over 5000 ft. Since ramp patches are less available to traditional harvesters because of overdevelopment and a recent ban on ramp collecting in the National Park, many people are trying to seed their own ramp patches. The EBCI Agricultural Extension Office hands out hundreds of ramp "sets" each spring. Accessibility to private patches is often severely guarded by family members—and with good cause.

Ramp festivals have been a major social and cultural event every year in North Carolina, Tennessee, and West Virginia. People drive hundreds of miles to attend every year, and some see it as a pilgrimage, or regional initiation for "foreigners" or outsiders of Appalachia. Local media, chambers of commerce, agencies for tourism, and national periodicals have all touted ramp festivals and ramp recipes in recent years. The exposure of ramps as a "mountain delicacy" has decidedly increased its demand. *Food Network TV* personalities like Emeril Lagasse and Rachael Ray have included ramps as a seasonal must-have for professional and amateur chefs. Top-chef restaurants in major US cities now offer ramps along with other exotic foods. Ramp recipes include fiddle heads, calamari, and truffles. The unique taste and powerful odor offer a different, yet enticing alternative to garlic, onions, or leeks.

As a result, ramps are being harvested in unparalleled numbers, much like the trend that occurred with mountain ginseng and goldenseal. The increased cost, reflecting marginal availability, as with Mountain icons—ginseng and white liquor—makes ramps almost too expensive for locals to purchase. Moonshine in the last two decades has risen from about $20 to $80 a gallon; ginseng can bring over $500 a pound; and ramps can easily run $40 a gallon—double the cost of only three or four years ago.

Websites can direct interested buyers to ramp farmers, primarily in West Virginia, where they can seasonally purchase cultivated ramps. Facemire, one of several distributors, was shipping ramps at almost $20 a pound in 2003. Another grower listed eighteen restaurants in the Chicago area as regular customers.

Many locals see the limited availability of ramps as just another sign of encroachment upon and destruction of Appalachian living. Several people interviewed said they had to harvest in places they couldn't reveal, most being on National Park land, yet they were willing to take the risk.

So What Do We Do?

The question of ramp sustainability is now an important topic. Forest Service botanists are unsure that current levels of ramp harvests are sustainable. They know that there is a need to monitor ramp populations and continue research regarding population decline in specific areas. Others are working to create gardens or farms to satisfy increasing demands for this important wild plant.

One woman and entrepreneur from Graham County, North Carolina, recently received international recognition for her work in producing "slow foods." Beverly Whitehead received a grant from the Cherokee Preservation Foundation to plant and process ramps for commercial sale. She has been very successful in marketing dehydrated ramps in ramp salt and ramp meal. She said, "Our bear hunters came up with the ideas. They traditionally take dried ramps and mix them with cornmeal to make cornbread in their camps. It's a local idea, based on an old local tradition" (2007). I can personally attest to the high quality of her products and encourage readers to visit her website and include these products in their culinary repertoire.

As are others in the area, she is concerned about the wholesale extinction of ramps and has thought of a way to provide people with the product without threatening the future of mountain ramps. She has fifteen people working with her, and she is a great example of Mountain resiliency and adaptability in a global economy.

Conclusion

Time changes things everywhere. Much of what I grew up with in Southern Appalachia has long been bulldozed down and privatized. Gaining access to medicinal plants and wild foods is becoming more difficult. Even people who have settled in the region within the past two decades are horrified at what looks like wholesale destruction of the land at the hands of money-seeking developers. This month in my home county, a confrontation at the courthouse between the "haves and have nots" will decide on a moratorium on housing developments.

As I've witnessed through my parent's difficult adjustment to changes in the land and the loss of much they knew as "Appalachian," the memories and connection to traditional foods like ramps will always bring us home.

Note

1. Note that in this paper, I am using the term *foodways* to refer to the ideas and practices surrounding the location, preparation, and consumption of food by a specific group—be it a family, ethnic group, or nation. Note also that this paper is built around a course I taught in Fall 2006, which preceded the SAS meetings where I presented the paper. I have made a few improvements to the paper as I presented it but have kept the "flavor" of the original.

Works Cited

Birringer, Marc, Clement Ip, Eric Block, Mihály Kotrebai, Julian F. Tyson, Peter C. Uden, and Donald J. Lisk. 2000. "Chemical Speciation Influences Comparative Activity of Selenium-Enriched Garlic and Yeast in Mammary Cancer Prevention." *Journal of Agricultural and Food Chemistry* 48(6): 2062–70.

E. Block. 2005. "Biological Activity Of Allium Compounds: Recent Results." *Acta Horticulturae* 688:41-57.

Calvey, E. M., K. D. White, J. D. Matusik, D. Y. Sha, and E. Block. 1998. "Allium Chemistry: Identification of Organosulfur Compounds in Ramp (*Allium tricoccum*) Homogenates." *Phytochemistry* 49:359-64.

Crellin, John K., and Jane Philpott. 1990. *A Reference Guide to Medicinal Plants*. Durham, NC: Duke University Press.

Jones, Almut G. 1979. "A Study of Wild Leek and the Recognition of Allium burdickii (Liliaceae)." *Systematic Botany* 4(1): 29-45.

Kauffman, Gary. 2001. "Forest Botanical Products: Maintaining Sustainability and Responding to Socioeconomic Needs in the Southern Appalachians." Unpublished report submitted to National Forest, Asheville, North Carolina.

Rattray, Diana. 2003. "Ramps and Wild Leeks: A Unique and Delicious Spring Jewel." About.com Guide. http://southernfood.about.com/cs/ramps/a/ramps.htm.

Walker, J. L., A. M. Silletti, and D. L. White. 2004. "Abundance of Ramps (*Allium tricoccum*) in the Southern Appalachians: Variability in Time and Space." Paper presented at the Association of Southeastern Biologists Annual Meeting, Memphis, TN, April 14-17.

Whanger, P. D. 2000. "Selenocompounds in Plants and Animals and their Biological Significance." *Journal of the American College of Nutrition* 21(3): 223-32.

Williams, Michael Ann. 1995. *Great Smoky Mountains Folklife*. Oxford, MS: University of Mississippi Press.

Zennie, Thomas M., and C. Dwayne Ogzewalla. 1977. "Ascorbic Acid and Vitamin A Content of Edible Wild Plants of Ohio and Kentucky." *Economic Botany* 31:76-79.

The Politics of Traditional Foodways in the Arkansas Delta

C. Laine Gates, Justin M. Nolan, and Mary Jo Schneider

Abstract

In response to skyrocketing rates of childhood obesity, state and federal policymakers have developed public school-based programs to fight "America's pandemic obesity problem." These programs have focused on promoting "healthy" lifestyles without attempting to explore the cultural or political factors that underlie childhood obesity. One such program was the cornerstone of former Arkansas Governor and Republican presidential contender Mike Huckabee's Health Arkansas Initiative, Arkansas' Act 1220 of 2003. The "BMI Initiative" (repealed in 2007) required annual school reporting of Body Mass Index scores. This paper examines BMI Initiative data and the creation of rural foodways—now considered traditionally African American and Southern in the Arkansas Delta—to demonstrate how African American views and behaviors conflict with dominant medical and political definitions of health. Policies that have arisen from public health constructions of obesity allow the politicization of body image for a culturally specific, hegemonic ideal of beauty that ultimately devalues Southern African American women and allows structural inequalities in health care to be effectively ignored.

Rates of obesity in America have reached unprecedented levels with as much as 65 percent of the adult population and 16 percent of children and adolescents now classified as overweight or obese (CDC 2006a). Obesity is pathologized by the medical community and the media and constructed as a primary global risk, effectively relegating obesity-related disease to the status of secondary risk. Not only do state and federal government groups support studies of obesity, but weight loss has become an American obsession. Popular television programs such as *Oprah* and *Dr. Phil* constantly feature discussions about the dangers of fat in American diets and about nutritional supplements and body surgical techniques that seem to offer solutions. Efforts from the $30-billion-a-year diet industry, however, focus not so much on health benefits from weight loss (substantiated mostly through reductions in diabetes) but emphasize improvements in self-confidence and good looks. The federal government provides nutritional guidelines and promotes physical activity, and the aims of public policy have followed suit, creating a rhetoric of individual responsibility in the war on fat. In an attempt to curb what is increasingly referred to as "America's pandemic obesity problem" (Tillotson 2004), state and federal policymakers are beginning to focus their attention on the role of nutrition education and physical activity in public schools. Public school students in Arkansas, Florida, Tennessee, Illinois, Pennsylvania, Texas, California, Delaware, Missouri, and West Virginia all have some sort of BMI testing (Wickline 2007, 2-B). However, instead of understanding obesity as a behavioral pathology, this paper views overweight as a normal biological and behavioral response to obesogenic conditions, as well as a socially constructed category closely tied to socioeconomic status (SES), environment, and ethnic identity. No matter how well intended, policies that promote a single culturally determined vision of a *healthy* lifestyle will not be sufficient to create effective change in providing for the health and well-being of public school students and their communities.

The terms *overweight* and *obese* refer generally to weights considered unhealthy, at which the likelihood for developing certain diseases and health conditions, such as hypertension, heart problems, failing hips and knees, and diabetes, is increased. While more accurate methods of determining body fat percentage exist, Body Mass Index, calculated from an individual's height and weight, is the measurement used most often in studies, since it is easy to calculate. An adult with a BMI falling between 25 and 29.9 is considered overweight, while an adult with a BMI of 30 or above is considered obese. The formula for categorizing BMI in children and adolescents differs slightly, placing individuals within specific percentiles referring to the relative position of the child's BMI number among children of the same gender and age. A child is considered "at risk for overweight" with a BMI falling between the 85th and 95th percentile, and "overweight" with a BMI equal to or greater than the 95th percentile (CDC 2006b). BMI statistics can be alarming, but it may not be the weight Americans sustain that causes long-term health problems as much as Americans' lack of exercise and balanced eating. Diet plans are largely unsustainable, and yo-yo dieting apparently causes increased rates of mortality.

With an overweight/obese rate of 63.1 percent, Arkansas ranks as the sixth fattest state in the nation (Levi, Segal, and Juliano 2006). In 2003, Arkansas became the first state to require all of its K-12 public school students to have an annual BMI assessment (Act 1220). The bill also set forth general rules regarding nutrition and physical activity aimed at providing "students with the skills, opportunities and encouragement to adopt healthy lifestyles." Among the key provisions of Act 1220 were the following requirements: "annually report each student's BMI to his or her parents and provide families with information about the importance of nutrition and physical activity, bar student access to food and beverage vending machines in elementary schools, and disclose food and beverage contract agreements, including revenues and expenditures." In addition, a Child Health Advisory Committee was created and, based upon the committee's recommendations, schools were subsequently also required, among other provisions, to "improve access to healthy foods in cafeterias, limit access to competitive foods (such as vended snacks and beverages) and ensure that products offered meet strict nutrition standards" (Act 1220 of 2003).

Headed by the Arkansas Center for Health Improvement, the Body Mass Index Initiative has resulted in a BMI database for approximately 97 percent of Arkansas' public school students. According to the nationally published results of the third-year study, "analysis of the BMI assessments reveals that the progression of the childhood obesity epidemic in Arkansas has been halted" (ACHI 2006b). This conclusion, however, seemed premature to the members of the 2007 General Assembly that replaced the Huckabee initiative with Act 201. This new act will require BMI measurements to be taken less frequently and will make it clear to parents that they have the right to refuse to have their children tested. Between 2003 and 2006, the overall BMI of Arkansas schoolchildren dropped from 38.1 percent to 37.5 percent—a decrease of only 0.6 percent. The largest drop in BMI, from 38.0 percent to 37.5 percent occurred from 2005 to 2006 (ACHI 2006b). By 2007, data seemed to indicate that the weight of children was either leveling off or increasing slightly. Furthermore, 80,000 Arkansas public school children were not tested, either because they refused to participate in the study or were absent from school when measurements were made. In year one of the study, 10 percent of those whose BMI could not be measured were listed as "child refused to be measured"; in years two and three, this reason accounted for 17 percent and 19 percent, respectively, of those who could not be measured. "Parent refused" was listed as between 21 percent and 24 percent during the three years of the study. An Arkansas Delta school nurse was quoted as saying that those who opted out were "usually the ones that need it" (Peacock 2006). Figures reported for the 2006-2007 school year showed that more than 50 percent of the students in four school districts (Bearden, Palestine-Wheatley, the KIPP Delta College Prepatory School in Helena-West Helena, and Strong-Huttig) were overweight (Wickline 2007, B-1). All of these school districts are in eastern Arkansas.

Upon closer examination of year-to-year data, it appears that the only groups that made (slight) progress were Caucasian males and females and Hispanic females. The two groups with the highest overweight/obese percentages, Hispanic males and African American females, saw little change. The percentage of Hispanic males classified as overweight/obese actually rose from 50 percent to 51 percent from 2004 to 2005, and then dropped back to 50 percent by 2006, while the percentage of African American females classified as overweight/obese remained at a relatively constant rate of 44 percent throughout all three years of the study. By the twelfth grade, all groups except African American females reached approximately the same population percentage of individuals classified as overweight/obese. All male subgroups' rates leveled off at 36 percent to 40 percent; Hispanic and Caucasian female rates declined to almost exactly 30 percent, while African American female rates jumped to approximately 45 percent (ACHI 2006a). Arkansas State Surgeon General Joe Thompson acknowledged that the rate of valid assessments had declined from 85 percent in 2005-2006 to 77 percent in 2006-2007 (Wickline 2007, B1).

With an overweight/obese population of approximately 64 percent concentrated mainly in the rural South, African American women nationwide are at a much higher risk for obesity than any other subgroup (Baturka, Hornsby, and Schorling 2000; Peralta

2003). Statistically, all of the following populations are most at risk for becoming overweight or obese: African Americans, females, those of low socio-economic status, residents of areas of ethnic segregation, residents of the rural South, and those with low levels of education (CDC 2006b; Chang 2006). According to the BMI Initiative data, rates of childhood obesity are highest in the Arkansas Delta where 25 percent of children are obese, compared with 16 percent nationwide (ACHSI 2006a). The Delta, with current and historical conditions marked by exploitation of human and agricultural resources, economic depression, and ethnic segregation, also has high rates of high blood pressure, diabetes, stroke, cancer, and heart disease. Low birth weights, high infant mortality rates, and infrequent medical care add to the region's poor health profile. Convenience stores outnumber supermarkets, and fruits and vegetables are relatively expensive. Delta diets are long on carbohydrates and sugars, short on vegetable, fruit, and dairy products, and fried potatoes make up one-third of all vegetables eaten (Champagne et al. 2004). Considering these risk factors, the Arkansas Delta can, in fact, serve as a microcosm for examining public health policy and the ways in which the numerous causes of obesity intersect to create unhealthy environments.

The portion of the Mississippi Alluvial Plain known as the Arkansas Delta encompasses ten million acres of land and is characterized by rich soils, plantation agriculture, ethnic and social stratification, and the most extreme and persistent poverty in the United States. The area's extensive waterways, while nourishing the soils, have also caused periodic flooding and swamp-related diseases. Droughts and boll weevils, enervating heat, deadly pests, pellagra, dysentery, malaria, typhoid, diarrhea, and hookworm combine to cause the Delta to be considered the least healthy section of America. The Delta remains fairly isolated today, which has also led to the region's "subcultural persistence in mass society" (Reed 1972). Today, the Delta's historic natural abundance is practically no more; the swamps and age-old aquifers have been drained, runoff from agricultural chemicals pollute the streams, and the once-lush forests have been clear-cut (Gatewood 1993). Such environmental devastation has long been linked to poor public health. Large-scale cultivation in the Delta relied on slave labor, and later, on black and white tenant farmers. To this day the region retains a significant portion of the state's African American population.

Historically, cotton is the main crop of the Delta, and as food selection for slaves was linked to the agricultural objectives of planters (Cobb 1992; Semmes 1996), widespread cultivation of a non-food, nutrient-intensive crop such as cotton had devastating and lasting effects on nutrition and health in the Delta. The cheapest and most easily preserved foods were pork and corn meal; thus, these became the core staples of the Delta diet. The plantation owners' leftovers, which provided slave rations, usually consisted of three to four pounds of fat pork and a peck of corn meal. Diets were later supplemented with rice and wheat products, but the availability of these products was limited. Pork, considered by doctors of the time to be *high energy* and thus suited to slaves and laborers, was ubiquitous, and every part of the animal was used—down to the feet and intestines. Methods of preservation were not uniform, but the meat was generally preserved with large quantities of salt, which significantly degraded its nutritional value. Other methods of preservation included smoking and pickling, and many slaves never consumed fresh meat. Certain types of poultry, mostly chickens, were also present, but were usually reserved for Sundays and special occasions, if they weren't sold. This limited availability (combined also, perhaps, with the preeminent symbolism of the chicken in West African culture) contributed to the view of chicken as a prestige food (Carney 1998; Semmes 1996).

In their own small garden plots, slaves grew turnips, sweet potatoes, cowpeas (black-eyed peas), cabbage, collards, pumpkins, okra, onions, and squash. Slaves also fished and hunted; the game most often caught included rabbit, opossum, and raccoon. Most of these foods, however, did not contribute significantly to diet, as they were usually sold or used by the plantation owners. Hunger and instances of nutritional disease are highest when vegetable consumption is lowest, and the vegetables that did make it on to the tables of slave families were cooked for hours with fat pork or bacon, greatly diminishing the nutritive content. *Potlikker*, the liquid left over from boiling vegetables and pork, retained some of the vitamins of the vegetables and was eaten with cornbread. The methods of cooking all available foods consisted of boiling or frying, most likely because the only utensils readily available were large cooking pots (Whitehead 1984; Semmes 1996).

The diets of African Americans did not improve after the Civil War. Freed slaves were landless and penniless and forced to work under a sharecropper system that was slavery in everything but name. Cotton was still king and still in competition with food production, and after years of harsh cultivation, soil qualities began to diminish, compounding the lack of dietary diversity. The diet of sharecroppers through the 1930s was almost identical to that of slave culture, and throughout the South, rural tenant farming families who owned no land and little more than the clothes on their backs, depended on landowners for meal, coffee, lard, flour, molasses, pork (often fatback), and the ever ubiquitous snuff and tobacco. When landowners had a store or commissary, prices were grossly inflated and credit charges were exorbitant. Corn remained the staple gain, eaten as hominy, roasting ears, or cornbread. Landowners typically supplied sharecroppers with a cabin and a garden plot, which provided some seasonal corn, Irish potatoes, collards, turnips, okra, peas, and beans. The combination of inadequate diet, heavy work, and excessive use of tobacco was often devastating.

In theory, landowners were not tied to working on a cotton farm and could diversify their diets by growing food. However, many land-owning farmers depended upon the sale of homegrown fruits and vegetables to buy staples. In Georgia during the 1920s and 1930s, vegetables probably made up "less than one-tenth of the food consumed by the mass of rural families" (Semmes 1996). These foodways still form the basis for the diets of many African Americans and Southerners and will prove very difficult to change, because, as Clovis Semmes (1996, 53) writes:

> Maladaptation to antibiosis is the dysfunctional way in which people may adjust to the constraints of exploitation in order to survive. Poor dietary habits that derive from adaptation to limited, inadequate, and nutritionally imbalanced food sources are examples. Adaptive responses are initially circumstantial and conditional but can become dysfunctional cultural habits. In the context of cultural hegemony, dysfunctional cultural habits are very hard to alter because they are frequently reinforced by the system of exploitation and subsequently have become tied to the identity of the group, whose members now view such habits as traditional.

While agricultural mechanization was hailed as an advance that would contribute significantly to public health (Levenstein 2003), it had the opposite effect in the Delta. Sharecropping all but disappeared, and the drastic reduction in cotton acreage due to federal legislation cut day labor employment as well (Cobb 1992). Food shortages increased in times of drought, and the New Deal relief programs increased the breakdown of home-production and dependence on store-bought foods. Younger generations who were lucky enough to be employed in federal programs like the WPA had far less time for and interest in gardening, while older generations still placed prestige on self-sufficient food production (Bennett, Smith, and Passin 1942). The diets of Delta people, in the past and today, were rich in carbohydrates and salt, and low in fresh, leafy vegetables. The change from a subsistence to cash economy meant that canned meats were substituted for wild game and fish and candy bars replaced home-canned fruits. Homegrown vegetables, wild greens, fish, and game such as squirrel, opossum, raccoon, and frogs became stigmatized (Bennett, Smith, and Passin 1942). This shift in foodways mirrored the mechanization of agriculture, further degradation of soil composition and a changing definition of success—from the possession of land to the possession of cash. Welfare payments, and the movement from commodities (ironically, surpluses given away to benefit the agriculture industry by driving up prices—still effectively the leftovers of plantation owners) to food stamps in the late 1960s, sealed the dependence on purchased (and less nutritious) foods (Levenstein 2003). In fact, this transition from agricultural surplus to food stamps is credited with causing conditions of starvation in the Delta by the 1960s. Participants in the federal food stamp program were required to purchase a month's supply of food stamps all at once, and most people who needed the stamps were not able to come up with sufficient funds to buy them. This crisis marks the first time in which poor black people in the Delta were the focus of national public health debate.

Following the Senate antipoverty committee's 1967 hearing in Jackson, Mississippi, Senator Robert Kennedy made a visit to the state's cotton-producing area where "thousands of black farm workers and sharecroppers" had been displaced by the push toward mechanization and crop-reduction. Although Representative Samuel Resnick of New York had visited the Delta nearly two years before and tried to call attention to "the desperation point of starving Negroes," it was Kennedy's well-publicized day-trip in the squalor of these communities that transformed black hunger into "a politically sexy issue" (Levenstein 2003). Soon after, numerous media organizations began publishing reports of desperate poverty and starvation, located mainly in the rural South, and the anti-hunger movement grew. While the media attention to conditions in the Delta did further the cause of separating food policy from the farm lobby and agricultural surplus, the health of the people of the Delta was ultimately manipulated only for political gain. Despite calls for increased aid and easing of food stamp requirements, President Johnson feared the implications that the enactment of such measures might have for Kennedy's presidential aspirations. House Agriculture Committee member Robert Poage of Texas was quoted as saying that he was "not going to help some deadbeat" and that "in the Book that most all of us accept it says somewhere, by the sweat of thy brow shalt thou eat bread." Sentiments such as these, which construct individuals as autonomous actors independent of social conditions, echo arguments that have long been made against social welfare programs. Even those politicians who professed loyalty to the anti-hunger cause were often revealed to be simply manipulating it for political gain. Despite President Nixon's 1969 vow to expand the food stamp program and "put an end to hunger in America for all time," he later was revealed to have stated in a meeting that very day, "Use all the rhetoric you need, as long as it doesn't cost money" (Levenstein 1973, 154).

Shortly after this statement, Nixon's social policy advisor Daniel Patrick Moynihan predicted events to come when he wrote of the need to examine "the remnant of pre-industrial problems, such as hunger and malnutrition, the onset of post-industrial problems, such as overeating, and the industrial era problems such as the toxic effects of prepared foods" (Levenstein 1973, 154). It was Moynihan's last suggestion that was to effectively end large-scale public attention to rural black hunger for a time and plant the seeds of the dominant political ideologies at work in the current obesity debate. Despite the intense national attention to black people's health through the 1960s, little good was accomplished in the Arkansas Delta, and the same social and political rhetoric is being replayed in the current obesity debate.

From the 1960s, declining death rates among African Americans from contagious disease paralleled an increasing death rate from degenerative and obesity-related diseases such as diabetes, cancer, and cardiovascular diseases (Semmes 1996). Modern foodways in the Delta reflect a tendency toward food behavior developed from the food insecurity of the antebellum South, combined with an increased dependence on the food available through social assistance programs. Foods available through social assistance, including foods available as part of the free and reduced public school lunch program, exhibit many of the same basic qualities as those available in the antebellum Delta. Those foods that are cheapest per calorie are those that are highest in fat and calories; healthier foods, such as fruits and vegetables, can increase a food budget by as much as 5,000 percent per calorie (Ulrich 2005). Public institutions, such as the historically poor and low-performing public schools of the Delta, and families facing financial troubles must stretch food budgets as far as possible. In fact, national public school lunches are still funded in part by agricultural surpluses—more leftovers (Sobo 1997).

As children, all humans learn to think of food as "given or withheld at the discretion of a donor," implying its possible uses as a means of control; government food assistance programs become a natural outgrowth of the power differentials among donors (the food and agriculture industries), the dominant cultural and sociopolitical ideology, and the hungry (Fitchen 1997). During the 1970s, middle-class fears over food safety and the use of pesticides eclipsed the issues of poverty and hunger within the media and public policy, creating ideals of clean food that resonate today in the nutrition, whole foods, and organic movement. Concurrently, public views turned against food assistance programs while participants were condemned for buying *pleasure* or *junk* foods instead of *necessities*. Reliance on high-fat, processed foods with little nutritive content can lead to obesity combined with malnourishment. For the first time, it was pointed out that low-income black women tended to weigh more than white women, the paradox of malnourished overweight was misunderstood, and the hunger lobby was seen as advocating "handouts for undeserving blacks." The growing middle-class concern over *pure* foods stigmatized those who were dependent upon lower-priced, high-calorie, processed *impure* foods, thus poor health was rationalized as the fault of the uneducated lower class due to the inability to "resist temptation and postpone gratification" (Levenstein 2003). A strong time preference fueled by urgent present need is often mistaken for a strong leisure preference and the indulgence of instant gratification over future needs (Douglas and Isherwood 1996).

While the mass media carry messages associating a slender body with health, attractiveness, and status, fast-food establishments are more prevalent in ethnically segregated, predominantly low-income black neighborhoods, and fast-food and snack advertisements are shown significantly more often during programming directed specifically toward African American children (Block, Scribner, and DeSalvo 2004, 10; Fitchen 1997; Morland et al. 2002, 1; Outley and Taddese 2006). These advertisements reflect an American preference for convenience foods, and consumption of heavily advertised, and thus high-status, foods can be interpreted as a way in which those of low socioeconomic status express membership within the larger society despite poverty. Not only do these foods carry connotations of status, they also, being cheaper per calorie, satisfy hunger for longer periods of time than do fruits and vegetables. Many parents express having trouble in denying hungry children access to these high status foods, particularly if they are unable to provide other, more expensive, commodities. Parents, who as children experienced hunger, do not want their own children to feel similarly deprived, and are, thus, more likely to indulge a child's requests for specific foods. Hunger is not simply a physical phenomenon, and high-status food consumption not only expresses group membership, it also stems feelings of psychological deprivation. The wealthy, however, can purchase these junk foods and healthier foods, as well. The poor can only afford to purchase one, and the increased psychological and physical satiety gained from higher-calorie, higher-status advertised foods often outweighs the higher nutritional content of more expensive foods (Fitchen 1997).

The increased dependence upon high-calorie, low-nutritive content foods carries implications specifically for mothers. Women of any socioeconomic status are likely to place nutritional needs of children above their own; however, the nutritional status of poor women is significantly compromised by this practice (Fitchen 1997; Whitehead 1984). Poor mothers have higher incidences of obesity and malnutrition than their higher-SES counterparts, and indeed, the other members of their own families (Roe and Eickwort 1973). Surveys indicate that although many rural Southern African American women are aware of the *healthy* lifestyle changes that are necessary in avoiding being classified as *overweight*, they are unable to make such changes. Long work hours, tight budgets, and minimal access to parks and recreational facilities (characteristic of ethnically segregated African American communities) all prevent changes in diet and physical activity, despite public education that stresses the benefits of such changes (Chang 2006; Baturka, Hornsby, and Schorling 2000). For many in such positions, there are more pressing matters than weight loss. In fact, for parents of low socioeconomic status, the weight of their children ranks among the least of their worries (Backett-Milburn et al. 2006). This could only compound the tendency for children of working parents with low SES to have fewer restrictions on and supervision of food habits. A state of perpetual financial inadequacy affects the structure of mealtimes, and in such conditions, parents allow children to decide when and what to eat (Fitchen 1997).

African American attitudes toward body image are frequently suggested as contributing to obesity. African American women are under less social pressure to be thin (Hawkins 2005). Particularly in rural areas, there is greater pressure to remain slightly overweight and to display self-acceptance, even in cases where women express personal dissatisfaction with body image, possibly illustrating the tension between African American ideals of a healthy body and white hegemonic ideals of a healthy body (Baturka, Hornsby, and Schorling 2000). African American women and girls are subjected to conflicting ideals of the body every day. Some black women express *preferring* a small-to-medium size body but identify a larger body as signifying better health (Liburd et al. 1999). Food insecurity has been shown to be positively linked specifically to overweight females (and not to overweight men) (Townsend et al. 2001), and the history of economic insecurity for African Americans in the Delta must certainly have created widespread food insecurity. One African American father in the Arkansas Delta refused to have his daughter take part in the BMI measurement saying, "Sissy's no different from anyone else in the family." African American respondents in a recent study published in *The Journal of General Internal Medicine* mentioned the importance of maintaining a perceived *healthy* weight in case of illness as a reason not to lose weight (Baturka, Hornsby, and Schorling 2000).

Extensive networks of friends and kin with whom families could trade and borrow from were of utmost importance in the days of the Delta's early colonization and remain important throughout the South today, particularly among those of low SES. (Fitchen 1997; Hughes 1997; Payne 1993; Whitehead 1984). Children of poor families are often specifically encouraged to share with others (Fitchen 1997). The importance of extensive kin networks relates to a positive view of higher weight in West African immigrant rural communities: "because kin share wealth, no one gets rich; because kin feed each other, no one becomes thin" (Sobo 1997). Health, prosperity, generosity, and connection are symbolized by plumpness, whereas a thin body implies a mean, hoarding, *socially-subversive* nature (Hughes 1997; Sobo 1997). An extensive support network reinforces physical and psychological health in periods of economic insecurity, and a healthy, plump physique is indicative of a caring and cared-for status. Contrary to the idea that an *overweight* body is a body out of control, for African American women it can be a way of affirming control over identity and a symbol of resistance against hegemonic white ideals of health and beauty.

While not as well publicized as many reports on the dangers of obesity, growing quantitative evidence supports an African American view of health as well. Overweight may, in fact, not be as deadly as the popular media claim. An influential study by the Centers for Disease Control and Prevention was shown to have incorrectly attributed thousands of deaths per year to obesity (McKay 2004). In a follow-up study published in *JAMA*, those who were classified by BMI as slightly *overweight*, but not *obese*, actually displayed a lower risk of death than those whose weight was classified as falling within the *normal* range (Flegal et al. 2005). A study published in the same issue of *JAMA* found that the risk factors for cardiovascular disease decreased "considerably over the past 40 years in all BMI groups." Rates of diabetes, the disease most often associated with overweight in the African American population, rose among all BMI classifications, not just overweight and obese (Gregg et al. 2005). Nagourney (2006) found that those who are overweight may fare better when critically ill. The fact remains, though, that African Americans of low SES in the rural South have life expectancies well below those of other subgroups in America. Arkansas ranks forty-third in overall life expectancy, and two of the Delta's counties, Crittenden and Phillips, made the top twenty list of the lowest life expectancies in the nation (Associated Press, September 12, 2006).

Ideas of health and foodways that are identified as belonging to Southern rural African Americans were developed during extended periods of food insecurity and are now operating in obesogenic environments of economic insecurity. Instead of focusing on the concept of an obesogenic environment, it may be more accurate to propose something more encompassing—an environment that is detrimental to total health, and not just weight. However, public policy continues to target weight and body image in order to benefit public health. Concepts of health influence the symbolism of the body, and "often ideas about the body and its health are ideological supports for conditions, such as class and gender inequalities" (Sobo 1997).

Nixon would be proud of Mike Huckabee's short-lived BMI Initiative—full of rhetoric and not a dime of funding for the implementation of public school health programs. Former Governor Huckabee's personal weight loss and his subsequent crusade against childhood obesity buy him quite a lot of national airtime. As a 2008 presidential hopeful, the social conservative didn't need to be a born-again Christian to create a platform of national interest; all he had to do was to be born again, 105 pounds lighter, and write a best-selling book about it (Peacock 2004). Huckabee, however, had considerable resources at hand in helping him to attain his weight goal, including a personal physician and even a bass boat (offered as incentive by his supportive wife).

The BMI Initiative in Arkansas mirrored the national obesity debate, as well as previous sociopolitical attention given to black health and black bodies in the South. Huckabee's rhetoric of improving the lives of Arkansas children carries bipartisan appeal, as does the stigma from overweight. Those on the conservative right can get behind this notion of "preventative healthcare" that curbing obesity supposedly accomplishes. Those African American children of low SES who are overweight are portrayed as ticking time bombs for draining publicly funded health care, a claim that sounds suspiciously like the criticisms of food assistance programs in the 1960s, as well as the worn-out arguments against social welfare programs in general. Those on the liberal left can get behind a constructed image of the obese as ignorant greedy consumers compromising the environment (even causing global warming) and eating up all kinds of resources to the detriment of the global community (Kolata 2006). It is worth noting that the initiative to repeal Huckabee's BMI initiative came from a member of the General Assembly from Rogers, Arkansas—the Ozarks, where the rate of obesity among public school children is lowest and concern over the negative effects of subjecting children to BMI measurements seems to be greatest.

The definition of *fat* or *obese* varies over time and space, and measures such as BMI are far less based in *science* than in the minds of a culture obsessed with weight loss and a slender body that signals social status, prosperity, beauty, and health (Kulick and Meneley 2005). Notions about health influence symbolism made through the body and the current framing of public health in terms of obesity devalue African American concepts of health and the body. Within economic structures defined by free market trade, theories of purity, in this case, food purity, are constructed as "techniques of selective exclusion." These categories of purity then serve as tests governing fairness in competition for status among individuals. Thus the white-middle-class emphasis on clean foods, which began in the late 1960s and 1970s, constructed the value judgment of *overweight* as indicative of an uneducated lower-class preference for *unclean* food sources, wherein overweight people are "judged as wanting in moral and intellectual stamina," having failed these tests of worth (Douglas and Isherwood 1996). The choices as they are framed by public policy and the media force the maxim "eat different, look different" in order to validate a specific culturally defined ideal. By focusing on obesity as the primary risk, instead of on the actual diseases that public policy is supposedly trying to prevent—wherein those targeted by policies must devalue their own cultural systems in order to be seen as taking responsibility for their own health—politicians and the media are not forced to truly examine the inequalities over which individuals have little power. Those inequalities do create not just an obesogenic environment, but an environment that compromises overall health. Although programs modeled on Arkansas' BMI Initiative are expanding nationally, we must ask whether or not these programs are ultimately exploiting the poor for political and social gain under the guise of humanitarian aims. Policymakers must ask themselves what it means to successfully implement health and nutritional policy, and they must also "answer for whom they do not invite to their table" (Douglas and Isherwood 1996). The Arkansas experience indicates that programs may do little in the final analysis to alleviate inequalities in dietary health.

Works Cited

Act 1220 of 2003: An Act to Create a Child Health Advisory Committee; to Coordinate Statewide Efforts to Combat Childhood Obesity and Related Illnesses; and to Improve the Health of the Next Generation of Arkansans. 2003. State of Arkansas, 84th General Assembly.

ACHI (Arkansas Center for Health Improvement). 2006a. Obesity and School Body Mass Index Initiative Database. http://www.achi.net/current_initiatives/obesity.asp

———. 2006b. Tracking Progress: The Third Annual Arkansas Assessment of Childhood and Adolescent Obesity (Nationwide Report on Arkansas 2005-2006 BMI Data. Little Rock: Arkansas Center for Health Improvement.

Associated Press. "Where You Live Can Decide How Long You Live." September 12. http://www.msnbc.com/id/14786805/

Backett-Milburn, K., W. J. Wills, S. Gregory, and J. Lawton. 2006. "Making Sense of Eating, Weight, and Risk in the Early Teenage Years: Views and Concerns of Parents in Poorer Socio-economic Circumstances." *Social Science & Medicine* 63(3): 624-35.

Baturka, N., P. P. Hornsby, and J. B. Schorling. 2000. "Clinical Implications of Body Image Among Rural African American Women." *Journal of General Internal Medicine* 15(4): 235-41.

Bennett, J. W., H. L. Smith, and H. Passin. 1942. "Food and Culture in Southern Illinois—A Preliminary Report." *American Sociological Review* 7(5): 645-60.

Block, J. P., R. A. Scribner, and K. B. DeSalvo. 2004. "Fast Food, Race/Ethnicity, and Income: A Geographic Analysis." *American Journal of Preventive Medicine* 27(3): 211-17.

Carney, G. O. 1998. *Baseball, Barns and Bluegrass*. Lanham, MD: Rowman and Littlefield.

CDC (Centers for Disease Control and Prevention). 2006a. "National Health and Nutrition Examination Survey 1999–2002." http://www.cdc.gov/nccdphp/dnpa/obesity/faq.htm#adults

———. 2006b. "Overweight and Obesity." http://www.cdc.gov/nccdphp/dnpa/obesity/

Champagne, C. M., M. L. Bogle, B. B. McGee, K. Yadrick, R. H. Allen, T. R. Kramer, P. Simpson, J. Gossett, J. Weber. 2004. "Dietary Intake in the Lower Mississippi Delta Region: Results of Our Delta Study." *Journal of the American Dietetic Association* 104(2): 199-207.

Chang, V. W. 2006. "Racial Residential Segregation and Weight Status Among U.S. Adults." *Social Science & Medicine* 63(5): 1289-1303.

Cobb, J. C. 1992. *The Most Southern Place on Earth: The Mississippi Delta and the Roots of Regional Identity*. New York: Oxford University Press.

Douglas, M., and B. C. Isherwood. 1996. *The World of Goods: Towards an Anthropology of Consumption*, rev. ed. London; New York: Routledge.

Fitchen, J. M. 1997. "Hunger, Malnutrition, and Poverty in the Contemporary United States." In *Food and Culture: A Reader*, edited by C. Counihan and P. Van Esterik. New York: Routledge.

Flegal, K. M., B. I. Graubard, D. F. Williamson, and M. H. Gail. 2005. "Excess Deaths Associated with Underweight, Overweight, and Obesity." *JAMA* 293(15): 1861-67.

Gatewood, W. B. 1993. "The Arkansas Delta: The Deepest of the Deep South." In *The Arkansas Delta: Land of Paradox*, edited by J. Whayne and W. B. Gatewood. Fayetteville: University of Arkansas Press.

Gregg, E. W., Y. J. Cheng, B. L. Cadwell, G. Imperatore, D. E. Williams, and K. M. Flegal. 2005. "Secular Trends in Cardiovascular Disease Risk Factors According to Body Mass Index in US Adults." *JAMA* 293(15): 1868-74.

Hawkins, B. D. 2005. "Cultural Attitudes and Body Dissatisfaction." *Black Issues in Higher Education* 21(25): 27.

Hughes, M. H. 1997. "Soul, Black Women, and Food." In *Food and Culture: A Reader,* edited by C. Counihan and P. Van Esterik. New York: Routledge.

Kolata, G. 2006. "For a World of Woes, We Blame Cookie Monsters." *New York Times*, October 29.

Kulick, Don, and Anne Meneley, eds. 2005. *Fat: The Anthology of an Obsession.* New York: Jeremy P. Tarcher/Penguin.

Levenstein, H. A. 2003. *Paradox of Plenty: A Social History of Eating in Modern America.* Berkeley: University of California Press.

Levi, J., L. M. Segal, and C. Juliano. 2006. "F as in Fat: How Obesity Policies Are Failing in America (TFAH Report.)" Washington: Trust for America's Health.

Liburd, L. C., L. A. Anderson, T. Edgar, and L. Jack, Jr. (1999). "Body Size and Body Shape: Perceptions of Black Women with Diabetes." *Diabetes Educator* 25(3): 382-88.

McKay, B. 2004. "CDC Study Overstated Obesity as a Cause of Death; Admitting Errors, Agency Expects to Revise Findings; Big Health Concerns Remain." *Wall Street Journal*, November, 23.

Moritz, R., and D. Thompson. "House Votes to Eliminate BMI." http://arkansasnews. com/archive/2007/01/30/News/340313.html

Morland, K., S. Wing, A. Diez Roux, and C. Poole. 2002. "Neighborhood Characteristics Associated with the Location of Food Stores and Food Service Places." *American Journal of Preventive Medicine* 22(1): 23-29.

Nagourney, E. 2006. "Outcomes: Heavy People May Beat Critical Illness More Often." *New York Times*, May 9.

Northrop, M. "Social Amplification of Risk in Relation to Obesity." http://www.kent. ac.uk/scarr/events/launchpapers.htm

Outley, C. W., and A. Taddese. 2006. "A Content Analysis of Health and Physical Activity Messages Marketed to African American Children During After-school Television Programming." *Archives of Pediatrics & Adolescent Medicine* 160(4): 432-35.

Payne, E. A. 1993. "What Ain't I Been Doing?" In *Women and the Delta*, edited by J. Whayne, and W. B. Gatewood. Fayetteville: University of Arkansas Press.

Peacock, L. N. 2006. "BMI Results Ballyhooed." [Electronic version]. *Arkansas Times*, August 31.

———. 2004. Too Fat! Governor Huckabee Blows the Whistle on the Weight of our State, Especially the Kids. *Arkansas Times*, October 14. http://arktimes. com/Articles/ArticleViewer. aspx?ArticleID=c22dbaa0-9d9e-4dcd-affc-b17a561b04b5

Peralta, R. L. 2003. "Thinking Sociologically about Sources of Obesity in the United States." *Gender Issues* 21(3): 5-16.

Reed, J. S. 1972. *The Enduring South: Subcultural Persistence in Mass Society*. Lexington, MA: D. C. Heath.

Roe, D. A., and K. R. Eickwort. 1973. "Health and Nutritional Status of Working and Non-working Mothers in Poverty Groups." Springfield, VA: National Technical Information Service.

Semmes, C. E. 1996. "*Racism, Health, and Post-industrialism: A Theory of African-American Health.*" Westport, CT: Praeger.

Sobo, E. J. 1997. "The Sweetness of Fat: Health, Procreation, and Sociability in Rural Jamaica." In *Food and Culture: A Reader*, edited by C. Counihan and P. Van Esterik. New York: Routledge.

Tillotson, J. E. 2004. "America's Obesity: Conflicting Public Policies, Industrial Economic Development, and Unintended Human Consequences." *Annual Review of Nutrition* 24(1): 617-43.

Townsend, M. S., J. Peerson, B. Love, C. Achterberg, and S. P. Murphy. 2001. "Food Insecurity is Positively Related to Overweight in Women." *Journal of Nutrition* 131(6): 1738-45.

Ulrich, C. 2005. "The Economics of Obesity: Costs, Causes, and Controls." *Human Ecology* 33(3): 10-14.

Wickline, Michael R. 2007. "Kids' Weight Problems Inching Up, State Reports." *Arkansas Democrat-Gazette*, September 11, B1-3.

Whitehead, T. L. 1984. "Sociocultural Dynamics and Food Habits in a Southern Community." In *Food in the Social Order: Studies of Food and Festivities in Three American Communities*, edited by M. Douglas. New York: Russell Sage Foundation.

Cherokee Snakebite Remedies

David Cozzo

> At first, serpents were not poison. No roots were poison, and man would have lived forever, but the sun passing over, perceived that the earth was not large enough to support all, in immortality, that would be born. Poison was inserted in the tooth of the snake, in the root of the wild parsnip, etc. And one of the first family was soon bitten by a snake and died. All possible means were used to bring the life but in vain. —John Howard Payne[1]

The tale above was related to missionary Daniel Butrick and transferred to playwright John Howard Payne early in the nineteenth century to explain why snakes carried such deadly poison and why a chance encounter with a snake, especially if it appears to be a poisonous one, instills mortal fear in the stoutest of hearts. It should come as no surprise that the rich tradition of Cherokee storytelling should contain an explanatory tale of the origin of snake poison, or that their vast pharmacopoeia would contain a wide array of remedies to treat one bitten by a snake. Here I will examine the historical record about these remedies and, through comparison with the findings of later researchers, attempt to clarify and identify the main remedies used by the Cherokee to treat snakebites.

Two poisonous snakes are encountered in the Southern Appalachian region: timber rattlesnakes (*Crotalus horridus*) and copperheads (*Agkistrodon contortrix*). The Cherokee have historically had ambivalent relationships with the rattlesnakes and a loathing for the copperheads. The rattlesnake was known as *u-tsa- na-ti* or "he has a bell" because of the alarm sounded by its rattle (Mooney 1900, 295). Rattlesnakes were approached with both a reverence for their power and a fear of their bite, as well as their association with the Thunder spirit. When Lightening, the youngest son of Thunder, was required by his father to play a stick ball match against his two older brothers, he chose for his adornment bracelets of copperheads and a necklace of a great rattlesnake to make himself appear fierce (Mooney 1900, 311). Mooney found that rattlesnakes were referred to as "the Thunder's necklace" and "to kill one is to destroy one of the most prized ornaments of the thunder god" (1900, 295). Rattlesnakes were considered the leaders of the snakes, and they epitomized the relationship of all snakes to the underworld (Fradkin 1990, 333). Olbrechts may have best captured the Cherokee attitude toward rattlesnakes:

> The Cherokee, like other Indians, has a great reverence for snakes in general, but for rattlesnakes in particular, and is careful never to offend one, even by word. In accordance with the principle often applied in the formulas of belittling a serious ailment, it is customary, when a man has been bitten by a snake, to announce that he has "been scratched by a briar." (Mooney and Olbrechts 1932, 177)

It was considered a foolish act to kill a rattlesnake because they were believed to have clan affiliations (Mooney 1900, 305). As with the blood law of the Cherokee, killing a member of a clan had to be avenged by the departed one's clan member. The balance had to be restored by taking the life of a member of equal value to the clan that had perpetrated the killing of one's affiliate. Therefore, if one killed a rattlesnake, the snake's clan would have to seek revenge on a member of the killer's clan. This rule was not limited to snake/

human interactions. It was said that snakes, ginseng, and deer were allies, all having exceptional powers, and that an action against one of them would be avenged by all of them (Mooney 1900, 294). Copperheads, on the other hand, were viewed as solitary creatures. They were generally despised and, since they had no comparable clan affiliations, they could be killed with impunity. The copperhead was known simply as *wo-di-ge a-sko-li*, or "brown head," an apt description that provided its common English name (Mooney 1900, 296).

The general therapy for treatment of snakebites consisted of both internal and external applications of a medicinal plant decoction. A portion of the decoction was imbibed, and the remainder was either blown or rubbed on the bite. The external application, whether blown or rubbed, was always performed in a counterclockwise direction, symbolizing the uncoiling of the serpent and the undoing of its intent. Dreams of snakebite were treated as an actual bite due to concern that, if untreated, inflammation and the symptoms of an actual bite would set in at the location of the dream-bite (Mooney 1891, 352).

James Adair was one of the earliest commentators on the range and efficacy of Cherokee snakebite remedies:

> I do not remember to have seen or heard of an Indian dying by the bite of a snake, when out at war, or a hunting; although they are then often bitten by the most dangerous of snakes—every one carries in his shot-pouch, a piece of the best snake-root, such as the *Seneeka*, or fern-snake-root,—or the wild hore-hound, wild plantain, St. Andrew's cross, and a variety of other herbs and roots, which are plenty, and well known to those who range the American woods, and are exposed to such dangers, and will effect a thorough and speedy cure if timely applied. When an Indian perceives he is struck by a snake,

> he immediately chews some of the root, and having swallowed a sufficient quantity of it, he applies some to the wound; which he repeats as occasion requires, and in proportion to the poison the snake has infused into the wound. For a short space of time, there is a terrible conflict throughout all the body, by the jarring qualities of the burning poison, and the strong antidote; but the poison is soon repelled through the same channels it entered, and the patient is cured. (1974, 247-248)

Some of the plants mentioned by Adair are easily identified by their common names. Others were vernacular names for plants that were later identified by other researchers as Cherokee snakebite remedies. The Seneeka is Seneca snakeroot, *Polygala senega*, which has its function indicated in its common name. The reference to the Seneca tribe in both the common and botanical names would also indicate an association with northern Iroquoian peoples, but documentation of this is not evident (Moerman 1998; Herrick 1995). Mooney claimed that the Cherokee did not use *P. senega* for snakebite, but for other unspecified illnesses and as a source of income in the commercial botanicals market (Cozzo 2004, 302). A later source that appears to cite it as a viable remedy may be referencing Adair, but it is not clear from the text (Hamel and Chiltoskey 1975, 55). Perhaps Mahoney's rendition of Cherokee physician Richard Foreman's relationship to P. senega can shed some light on the ambiguity associated with its use for snakebite:

> Much has been written with regard to its virtue in the cure of the bite of the snake; we never used it for this purpose, believing that the remedies prescribed for the treatment of animal poisons are superior to this root; but should a case occur where this root was at hand, and the remedies prescribed under that head could not be

obtained, we would give it a fair trial; the mode of using it internally in tea or decoction, and externally, to the wound. (1857, 245)

The fern snake root mentioned by Adair appears to be *Botrychium virginianum*, the rattlesnake fern. While the vernacular name "rattlesnake fern" could be attributed to an association with the rattle of a rattlesnake because of the erect nature of its fertile frond, Olbrechts claimed that it was the primary remedy for a dream-snakebite. The Cherokee had an elaborate system of disease diagnosis associated with the dream world (Mooney and Olbrechts 1932, 35-37), and a dream of being bitten by a snake was treated as an actual bite. If the dream-bite was left untreated, the victim would eventually develop swelling and ulcers on the spot, just as if it were an actual bite (Mooney 1900, 295; Mooney and Olbrechts 1932, 176). Rattlesnake fern was applied to both a dream-bite and, in the absence of a superior remedy, was an acceptable remedy for an actual bite (Mooney and Olbrechts 1932, 177; Cozzo 2004, 337).

Wild horehound may be more difficult to identify than other remedies mentioned by Adair. Mahoney says that wild "hoarhound" is *Eupatorium pilosum* and that it is "too well known to need description" (Mahoney 1857, 227), but he makes no mention of it being used as a snakebite remedy. However, it is very closely related to and bears a close resemblance to the species *Ageratina altissima* (formerly *Eupatorium rugosum*), a common species in the North Carolina mountains, which is one of several plants known as white snakeroot. Banks identified *Lycopus virginicus* by the common name "water horehound," which the Cherokee boiled in milk and gave to a dog that had been bitten by a snake (2004, 94). One local man in the mountains of North Carolina identified *L. virginicus*, also known as bugleweed, as "meadow horehound," and his description of its use matched that described by Banks (personal communication, June 15, 2005). Mooney also mentioned that L. virginicus was used for snakebites, but he gave no indication of its application (Cozzo 2004, 206). Such evidence would suggest that L. virginicus is the most likely candidate for the remedy described by Adair as "wild horehound."

Adair's wild plantain was most likely *Cacalia atriplicifolia*, the pale Indian plantain. While not specifically mentioned for use as a snakebite remedy, Mooney (1891, 326) did tout its virtues as a poultice for drawing toxins out of wounds: "…held in great repute as a poultice for cuts, bruises, and cancer, to draw out poisonous matter. The bruised leaf is bound over the spot and frequently removed." St. Andrews cross, the last of the plants specifically named by Adair, is the common name for *Hypericum hypericoides*, so named because the four-parted flowers resemble an x-shaped cross. The legend of St. Andrew suggests that, when he was crucified, he asked that it be done on a cross of a different shape from that of Jesus. This x-shaped cross is also the basis for the crossed bars on the Confederate flag. No other researchers mentioned this plant for snakebite; however, Banks did find that it was used for its ability to reduce fevers, a function that would be beneficial for systemic inflammation caused by snakebite (2004, 78). Two other species of Hypericum are used in traditional Chinese medicine as remedies for snakebite (Houghton and Osibogun 1993), suggesting that the genus may have some inherent efficacy. While Adair does not mention their names, he does indicate that, "a variety of other herbs and roots, which are plenty" could be applied to a snakebite. Such a statement would indicate that he would find no flaw with the reports of later researchers who added many more plants to his list.

The next treatment of Cherokee remedies appears to have come from the French botanist Palisot de Beauvois, sent to the Southeast in 1796 to reestablish the fur trade among the Creeks and Cherokees.

De Beauvois recorded the following information in his notes in what he called a "table of snakebite remedies," although not really a table in a contemporary sense:

> Table of Remedies and Plants Employed by the Cherokees Against Snakebite
>
> In the first moment of the bite they use three kinds of remedies: the suction which is always the most effective when it is possible to employ, or chewed tobacco applied to the wound or cannon powder to which one sets afire.
>
> Once at home they use three plants.
>
> One, a kind of helianthus which I have not yet well determined.
>
> The very milky root of the *prenanthes alba* or its varieties as well as all lactuca. The bark root of tulipier; in the most serious cases all of the plants are employed in infusion.
>
> In the course of the treatment they use the root of *Spiraea trifoliata*. Therein they find the double advantage of being strongly purged and of abundant vomiting.
>
> It is good which in general they make use of in all sicknesses the plants of the family composita and of the bark of several trees and plants found in large numbers in North America. (Anderson 1984)

The tobacco mentioned by de Beauvois was most likely *Nicotiana rustica*, the "old tobacco" of the Cherokee and the primary tobacco used in ritual and medicine (Cozzo 2004). Mooney had the following to say about *N. rustica*:

> Tobacco was used as a sacred incense or as the guarantee of a solemn oath in nearly every important function—in

> binding the warrior to take up the hatchet against the enemy, in ratifying the treaty of peace, in confirming sales or other engagements, in seeking omens for the hunter, in driving away witches or evil spirits, and in regular medical practice. It was either smoked or sprinkled on the fire, never rolled into cigarettes, as among the tribes of the Southwest, neither was it ever smoked for the mere pleasure of the sensation. (Mooney 1900, 424)

Nicotiana rustica is a much stronger tobacco, possessing as much as eight times the nicotine content of the introduced *N. tobacum*, the species prevalent in the commercial trade (Haley, Gardner, and Whitney 1924; Idris et al. 1998). Besides applying tobacco to the bite, the person treating the bite would also hold tobacco in his mouth to counteract the poison sucked out of a bite (Mooney and Olbrechts 1932, 241).

The *Helianthus* mentioned by de Beauvois could have been one of a number of native sunflowers or sunflower-like plants. I take exception with Anderson's informant who dismissed its potential out-of-hand (Anderson 1984). There are as many as sixteen species of Helianthus and numerous species of related yellow-flowered members of the family *Asteraceae* growing in the Southern Appalachian Mountains (Smith 1998, 190-192). The edible sunflower, *Helianthus annuus*, has been recorded as a snakebite remedy in the Southwest, being employed by the White Mountain Apache and Zuni (Moerman 1998, 257). This would indicate some degree of efficacy for that particular species, not to mention other members of the genus. Mooney recorded that a decoction of the roots of *Rudbeckia fulgida*, a type of black-eyed Susan that resembles a small sunflower, was used as a wash on snakebites (Mooney 1891, 327). Perhaps this plant, or a closely-related one, was the unknown Helianthus observed by de Beauvois.

In keeping with his praise of the medicinal qualities of the family Asteraceae (he refers to it as *composita*), de Beauvois highlighted *Prenanthes alba* and the genus *Lactuca*. Several species of Prenanthes are common to the Southern Appalachians, some more common than *P. alba*, which is found only in a few counties in western North Carolina (Radford, Ahles, and Bell 1968, 1020). However, de Beauvois did indicate that the "varieties" of P. alba were suitable substitutes. No other researchers corroborated the use of either Prenanthes or Lactuca for snakebite, but the common name of "rattlesnake root" applied to P. alba and some related species of Prenanthes would indicate a reputation for some degree of efficacy. In the Cherokee ethnobotanical classification system, P. alba is considered a small folk species of the folk genus *da ye wa*, or "it sews itself up." The large folk species of this genus is *Cacalia atriplicifolia*, mentioned above as a potential snakebite remedy.

The root bark of the tulip poplar, *Liriodendron tulipifera*, got a passing mention by de Beauvois (as *tulipier*), but was highly touted for a range of conditions and wound-healing capacity by both Olbrechts and Banks (Cozzo 2004, 78). One of Olbrechts' many claims included its use as a suitable substitute for the rattlesnake fern, *Botrychium virginianum*, in cases of snakebite. A decoction of the root bark was blown over the patient and rubbed directly on the site of the bite (Mooney and Olbrechts 1932, 177). Mahoney applied tulip poplar specifically for the bite of a copperhead:

> I have known the bite of the copperhead cured in the following manner: Immediately apply to the wound, tobacco, which has been perfectly wet in vinegar, and, as soon as it can be prepared give a strong decoction of the yellow-poplar root bark, and bathe the wound frequently with the same. (1857, 99)

The Spiraea trifoliata mentioned by de Beauvois is an old name for *Portheranthus trifoliata*, also known as Indian Physic or American Ipecacuanha. The common names refer to its strong purging and emetic qualities. Again I take exception with Anderson's informant who suggests that P. trifoliata was used as "a calming or soothing agent." Mooney found mixed responses to the use of this plant, some claiming that it was useful for severe bowel complaints, others claiming that it was too toxic to take internally (1891, 326). As mentioned above, de Beauvois found that those who partook of this medication were "strongly purged and of abundant vomiting," neither of which should be considered calming or soothing. However, it is reported to be a safe and efficient emetic (PDR 2004, 460) and would have served the purpose ascribed to it by de Beauvois.

Emesis was an important aspect of Cherokee snakebite therapy, especially in cases of a dream-snakebite. Dreaming of snakes causes the dreamer's saliva to become *spoiled*, a serious medical condition among Southeastern Indians. Saliva was considered to be associated with the primary soul, located in the head, in the Cherokee humoral system (Witthoft 1984; Fogelson 1982; Cozzo 2007). Natural or intentional disturbance in the state of saliva had to be addressed, usually in the form of an emetic. The Swimmer manuscript (Mooney and Olbrechts 1932, 198) contains an elaborate formula for such an emetic. It included a decoction of two types of rush, the soft-stemmed bulrush (*Schoenoplectus tabernaemontani*) and the soft rush (*Juncus effusus*), wood vetch (*Vicia caroliniana*), and poison ivy (*Rhus radicans*) found growing on the east side of a poplar tree. Another species mentioned in the formula, *Coronilla varia*, or crown vetch, may have been a misidentification. According to some sources, it was not introduced to this country from Asia until the 1950s (http://www.wvdnr.gov/Wildlife/DirtyDozen.shtm), making it an unlikely candidate for inclusion in a Cherokee formula, much less having been ascribed a Cherokee name. There are, however, local populations in the North Carolina mountains near present-day Cherokee, so if there was a much earlier introduction, it may have been included in the Cherokee pharmacopoeia.

The myth of the origin of snake poison was not the only mention of snakebite in the Payne/Butrick papers. The papers also contained a clear description of how to treat a bite that included some Cherokee names for the plant remedies:

> They (Thunders) were directed to a weed in the woods the top of which is a rattle like that of a rattlesnake and take the root. It must be dug in the winter when the top is dry. Also to another root the blossom of which has something rising out of it like a rattlesnake's tooth. The third the top smells like a snake. The fourth has one round slim stem grows up high and a branching flower at the top. The fifth is called Senica snake root called the first snakes tail (*I nv tv ka to ki*) . . . second owl's head (*u gu gu sko*), third (*A yv ta wi gi*) 'some round thing mashed'. Fourth (*kv ne li ta*), anything with young. Fifth (*u nv ste tsv sti ki*), senica snake root.
>
> All pounded together some of the compound is taken in the mouth, and with it in the mouth the place is sucked which was bitten. Snake doctors always kept this compound by them. (Payne, n.d. Vol. 3, 82)

Snake's tail (*I nv tv ka to ki*) most likely refers to *Prunella vulgaris*, also commonly known as heal-all or self-heal. The Cherokee name refers to the dried flower head, which does indeed resemble the erect tail of a rattlesnake. Mooney recorded two names for P. vulgaris (Cozzo 2004, 237): *inatu gataga* ("snake tail") and *inatu wasitsu* ("snake rattle"). Both names provide evidence that the species referred to by Butrick is, indeed, P. vulgaris. Prunella vulgaris is considered a panacea by both Chinese and Native American herbal practitioners, and current research shows it to be the highest known source of rosmarinic acid, a powerful antioxidant (Duke 1992, 158). Mooney identified owl's head (*u gu gu sko*) as *Pedicularis canadensis*, commonly known as lousewort. The name, which Mooney recorded as *ugukuska*, stems from *uguku* ("the hooting owl") and ("head") and refers to the appearance of the flowering head (Cozzo 2004, 283). The observation that "the blossom of which has something rising out of it like a rattlesnake's tooth" refers to the individual flowers, which are curved in a manner resembling a snake's fang.

The plant whose "top smells like a snake" had been a mystery to me before finding this reference. Olbrechts recorded a plant that he glossed as "the (plant) which is called: snake's odor"; however, he was unable to provide a botanical species to coincide with this distinctive name (Cozzo 2004, 237). But Butrick's supplying the Cherokee name *a yv ta wi gi* ("some round thing mashed") may solve this mystery. Mooney recorded the name *ayutawigi* for *Thalictrum dioicum*, commonly known as early meadow rue, and glossed it as "it bursts" due to the tendency of the stalk to burst when pressure was applied (Cozzo 2004, 217). This coincides nicely with Butrick's gloss of "some round thing mashed." It was common for Cherokee plants to have more than one name depending on consensus or lack of consensus by the informants. In this instance, there may have been more than one salient feature that determined the name(s) for *T. dioicum*. My own experience suggests that the members of the genus Thalictrum do have a musky odor, but comparing that smell to a poisonous serpent will have to wait until there is an opportunity for proper confinement of the serpent.

The reference to *kv ne li ta*, ("anything with young") is, again, very similar to the name of a plant recorded by Mooney as *ganelita* ("pregnant"). This was one of the Cherokee names for *Angelica venenosa* or hairy angelica (Cozzo 2004, 231). The reference to pregnancy or having young may be descriptive of the swollen leaf nodes common to members of the family Apiaceae, which are especially prominent on *A. venenosa*.

Butrick's fifth, and last, plant in this formula may have been misidentified. He refers to it as "Senica snake root," the common name applied the *Polygala senega* or the "Seneeka" mentioned by Adair. However, the Cherokee name supplied by Butrick (*u nv ste tsv sti ki*) bears no resemblance to the name recorded by Mooney for P. senega (*uyugili*), but it is very close to *unastetstiya* ("very small root"), the name Mooney recorded for *Aristolochia serpentaria* or Virginia snakeroot (Cozzo 2004, 290). Olbrechts claimed that *A. serpentaria* was a viable substitute for rattlesnake fern (*Botrychium virginianum*) or tulip poplar (*Liriodendron tulipifera*) when treating a snakebite that occurred in a dream (Mooney and Olbrechts 1932, 177). As both the common name and specific epithet suggest, A. serpentaria had a reputation as a snakebite remedy and would most likely have been included in the Cherokee repertoire on the occasion of an actual snakebite.

I am ambivalent about including James Mahoney's *The Cherokee Physician; or, Indian Guide to Health* (1857) in this work as it gives no background on the Cherokee practitioner, Richard Foreman, nor does it really discuss Cherokee ethnomedicine. However, it does use the Cherokee names for some illnesses and remedies, indicating some familiarity with Cherokee language and concepts. But even these are placed in a framework of mid-nineteenth-century, western-biomedical understanding of medicine and physiology. So while I include excerpts from Mahoney's work here, I urge the reader to view the authenticity of his portrayal of Cherokee ethnomedical practices with a healthy dose of skepticism.

Mahoney's first protocol for snakebite was to purge the patient with a powerful emetic, preferably *lobelia* (most likely *Lobelia inflata* or Indian tobacco, the preferred emetic of nineteenth century Thomsonian physicians). This treatment was followed by liberal doses of an infusion of the root of "rattle-snake's master," which he claimed could be harmlessly imbibed in large doses. This treatment would "cure the bite of the copper-head or rattle-snake, or any other poisonous reptile" (1857, 98). The plant commonly known as rattlesnake master is *Eryngium yuccafolium*, and Mahoney's description suggests that this is the case. He also claimed that "it is the most powerful and certain remedies for snake-bite now known" (1857, 267). It should be noted that Mooney claimed that starry campion, *Silene stellata*, was locally known in the Southern Appalachian region as rattle-snake's master, and he recorded the Cherokee name for Eryngium yuccafolium as *selikwaya*, or "green snake," because of the appearance of the leaves. However, Mahoney's description is more suited to E. yuccafolium than S. stellata, and in this case, I am confident that his reference is to the former.

Mahoney's alternative treatment was a bit more elaborate:

> Apply the ligature or bandage and administer the emetic above as directed, and after the operation of the emetic, give a tea of piny-weed root freely. For an external application to the wound, make a plaster to the wound of equal quantities of salt, tobacco, indigo, and hog's-lard; pulverize the tobacco, indigo, and salt, then mix all the articles together and apply it in the form of a poultice. A free usage of spirits, such as whisky, brandy, etc., will be found of great benefit in all cases of bites or stings. I have ascertained from personal observation, that a person when intoxicated, cannot be poisoned by the bite of a snake. Many lives have been saved by the free use

of whisky and red pepper; indeed, I believe that whisky alone will save life in many instances, when the bite would prove fatal if an active remedy was not resorted to immediately. (1857, 98-99)

The "piny-weed" referred to in this protocol was most likely *Hypericum gentioides*, commonly known as pineweed due to its resemblance to a small pine tree. Mooney identified pineweed as such and commented that the Cherokee name, *natsiyusti* ("like a pine tree"), was based on the same observable quality (Cozzo 2004, 170). Mahoney recorded an almost identical Cherokee name (*no-tse-e-yau-stee*) in *The Cherokee Physician* and claimed that it "will cure the bite of a copper-head, or rattle-snake" (1857, 267). This is a close relative of the St. Andrew's cross (*Hypericum hypericoides*) mentioned by Adair and could very well have a similar biochemical profile that would prove effective against snakebites. Whisky would have been an adopted remedy, but its remedial potential was well known to the Cherokee by the mid-nineteenth century.

Other herbal snakebite remedies mentioned by Mahoney include striped blood-wort, Indian *sanide* (sanicle?), mountain dittany, and the common green plantain (1857, 99). Stripped blood-wort may be stripped gentian (*Gentiana villosa*), blood-wort being a common name for closely related members of the Gentian family in the British Isles used to purify the blood (Allen and Hatfield 2004, 194). One of the North American common names is *Sampson snakeroot* (Crellin and Philpott 1990, 378). Mahoney suggests applying the bruised leaves to the bite and taking a tablespoon of the juice of the plant every few minutes. Mahoney's mention of Indian sanide may be a misprint by the publisher. Sanicle would easily by misread as sanide if the "c" and "l" were combined as one letter. This would make more sense, as North American members of the genus Sanicula are commonly referred to as black snakeroot (Crellin and Philpott 1990, 99) and both Mooney (Cozzo 2004, 182) and Banks (2004, 83) make mention of *Sanicula canadensis* as a species of sanicle known to the Cherokee. However, neither mentions *S. canadensis* as a snakebite remedy. But it is also possible that this plant is not in the genus Sanicula at all. Indian sanicle is one of many common names for *Ageratina altissima*, also known as white snakeroot or white sanicle (Panter and James 1990). Mountain dittany is the common name for *Cunila origanoides*, a member of the mint family that fits Mahoney's description. He claimed, "It is very good for snake bite. In this case, the tea should be drank freely, and the bruised leaves applied to the wound." A 1687 account of the tribes of Virginia referred to this plant as not a true dittany, but "mountain calamint," and claimed it would not only cure the bite of a rattlesnake but that the very smell of this plant would cause the snake to die (Hoffman 1964). The common green plantain, *Plantago major*, is a well-known wound healer, and Banks (1953, 101) claimed it was used as a Cherokee remedy for bee stings. According to Mahoney, "Bruise the herb and root and apply it to the wound, and at the same time take the expressed juice or tea freely." (1857, 99)

James Mooney, for all his writing on Cherokee culture, provided surprisingly little information about snakebite remedies. His primary discussion on the topic concerned *Silene stellata*, commonly known as starry campion or, locally in Southern Appalachia, rattlesnake's master (Mooney 1900, 295). He claimed that "the juice is held to be a sovereign remedy for snakebites, and it is believed that even the deadliest snake will flee from one who carries a small portion of the root in his mouth." The dried root was beaten and made into a poultice or chewed and applied to the bite. This application would cure the bite if applied within twenty-four hours, even if yellow liquid was seeping from the puncture.

In his field notes, Franz Olbrechts claimed it was another member of the Silene genus that was a primary snakebite remedy: *Silene virginica* or fire pink (Cozzo 2004, 150). As with Mooney's description of the use of Silene stellata, Olbrechts claimed that chewing on a piece of the root would ward off snakes. In case of an actual bite, the juice produced by chewing the root would be blown on the site in a counterclockwise direction. It is highly unlikely that these two species were confused by Mooney and Olbrechts. Even though they are classified in the same genus, the starry campion has white, fringed flowers, and the fire pink has red, showy flowers, making them easily distinguishable from each other, even to the untrained eye. However, their close botanical relationship would indicate that they may share biochemical similarities and were both efficacious against snakebites.

The other snakebite remedy discussed by Mooney was basswood (*Tilia americana*), the bark of which was chewed and placed on the site of a bite. He surmised that its usefulness might come from its association with the Thunder spirit and the fact that the basswood had a reputation of being immune from lightning strikes (Mooney 1900, 295). Banks added that a cold tea of the bark was drunk and applied externally when a dog was bitten by a snake (2004, 77).

Banks mentioned two new species not encountered by earlier ethnographers. The roots of hog peanut (*Amphicarpa bracteata*) could be used in place of chewing tobacco as a general snakebite remedy (2004, 67), and the roots of cocklebur (*Xanthium strumarium*) were chewed for a rattlesnake bite (2004, 113). In the case of *A. bracteata*, the root was brewed and blown on the bite accompanied by a song and a prayer. Cocklebur has a reputation in the Appalachian region as a snakebite remedy, but the part used was primarily the leaves instead of the roots (Crellin and Philpott 1990, 163-164).

Two other plants, hepatica or liverleaf (*Hepatica acutiloba*) and walking fern (*Asplenium rhizophyllum*) were combined in a decoction and used as an emetic for dreams of snakes (Banks 2004, 20), but it is not clear from the source if this was used to treat a dream snakebite or just for disturbing dreams of snakes. *Asplenium rhizophyllum* was known as *inatu ganka*, or "snake's tongue" in Cherokee, because of the resemblance of this small fern to a serpent's tongue (Cozzo 2004, 335).

In the opening epigraph, it was said that when poison was inserted into the tooth of the serpent, it was also placed in the wild parsnip. The wild parsnip mentioned here is not the feral relative of the European parsnip, *Pastinaca sativa*, but *Cicuta maculata*, also known as water hemlock or spotted cowbane. This is the most toxic plant in the Northern temperate zone, with the roots being the most toxic portion (Westbrooks and Preacher 1986, 128). It was used by the Cherokee primarily for conjuring, poisoning, and suicide, but there is also a reason it should be included in an article on snakebite remedies. According to Mooney, "Before starting on a journey, a small piece of the root is sometimes chewed and blown upon the body to prevent sickness, but the remedy is almost as bad as the disease, for the snakes are said to resent the offensive smell by biting one who carries it" (1900, 425). So, in this instance, one who used *Cicuta maculata* for the prevention of disease would also be well served to carry at least one of the roots reputed to repel snakes, thus avoiding two potential maladies on their journey. Or the traveler could rely on the method mentioned in the Payne/Butrick (n.d., Vol. 1, 21) papers: "Hunters, also, would wave their leggings and moccasins over fire, to secure protection from snakes."

Historical ethnobotany is rarely an exact science. The earliest ethnographers had limited knowledge of native languages or indigenous botanical classification systems, and their botanical sophistication would have applied to European species at best (Merrill and Feest 1975). Unless voucher specimens were collected and have been examined, it is impossible to verify the identity of plants described in historical works to the precise botanical species. However, the Cherokee were visited and written about by so many ethnographers, that speculation on the botanical species under consideration can be promoted with a high degree of certainty. What makes the Cherokee case unique is the linguistic evidence incorporated with botanical descriptions or species identification. The Cherokee names provided by Butrick or Mahoney can be cross-referenced with the linguistic materials collected by Mooney. Most of the plant specimens that he collected were identified to species by his colleagues at the Smithsonian Institution, some of the most capable botanists of his day. Olbrechts, also working under the aegis of the Smithsonian Institution, would have the same botanical support system as Mooney. Banks approached his research from both a botanical and ethnographic perspective, providing scientific, common, and Cherokee names. Such a treasure trove of ethnobotanical knowledge allows the descriptions of the past to be examined in a new light.

This paper clearly demonstrates that, as Adair noted, the Cherokee employed quite a number of remedies to deter and cure snakebites, many containing some reference to a snake in their common English names. Indeed, if some of the obscure references are counted, those referenced in this article are impressive: Seneca snakeroot (*Polygala senega*), rattlesnake fern (*Botrychium virginianum*), rattlesnake root (*Prenanthes alba*), Virginia snakeroot (*Aristolochia serpentaria*), rattlesnake master (*Eryngium yuccafolium* and *Silene stellata*), black snakeroot (*Sanicula canadensis*), Sampson snakeroot (*Gentiana villosa*) and white snakeroot (*Ageratina altissima*). This would indicate the endurance of indigenous knowledge as it was transmitted to their Euro-American neighbors.

Several remedies also exemplify the homeopathic principle ("like cures like") known to Western herbalists as the "doctrine of signatures." According to this doctrine, an observable quality in a medicinal remedy is indicative of which symptoms it will alleviate. Typically, the feature under consideration is morphological in character, but it may also be the color, aroma, or habitat that indicates a remedy's usefulness.

Mooney relates the concept to the Cherokee ethnomedical system in this manner:

> Cherokee medicine is an empiric development of the fetich idea. For a disease caused by a rabbit the antidote must be a plant called "rabbit's food," "rabbit's ear," or "rabbit's tail;" for snake dreams the plant used is "snake's tooth;" for worms a plant resembling a worm in appearance, and for inflamed eyes a flower having the appearance and name of "deer's eye." A yellow root must be good when a patient vomits yellow bile, and a black one when dark circles come about his eyes, and in each case the disease and the plant alike are named from the color. A decoction of burs must be a cure for forgetfulness, for there is nothing that will stick like a bur; and a decoction of the wiry roots of the "devil's shoestring" must be an efficacious wash to toughen the ballplayer's muscles, for they are almost strong enough to stop the plowshare in the furrow. (1900, 329)

In the case of the Cherokee snakebite remedies, *Prunella vulgaris*, *Botrychium virginianum*, and *Polygala senega* all have portions that are held erect and resemble the rattle of the rattlesnake. Also, as mentioned above, the flower of *Pedicularis canadensis* resembles the fang of a rattlesnake, *Thalictrum dioicum* has an odor like that of a snake, and *Asplenium rhizophyllum* resembles the tongue of a snake. But, from the small ratio of "signature" plants in relation to the whole, it appears unlikely that this would indicate selection criteria for determining snakebite remedies. While such a "signature" would serve as a potent mnemonic device for transmitting and retaining valuable cultural knowledge, stating, as Mooney does, that such an identifying feature must be present does not hold up when the whole range of potential remedies are considered.

Perhaps it should not be surprising that the Cherokee have so many remedies for snakebites. Snake venom is a complex cocktail of modified digestive proteins that have a direct effect on blood coagulation, the nervous system, the heart, and skeletal muscles (Koh, Armugam, and Jeyaseelan 2006). The Southern Appalachian homeland of the Cherokee is one of the most botanically diverse temperate bioregions on the planet. The combination of the seriousness of a snake's bite and the wide range of available potential medicines would, in Adair's words, lend itself to the knowledge of, "a variety of herbs and roots, which are plenty, and well known to those who range the American woods."

Note

1. John Howard Payne Papers, Vol. 3, 82. n.d. Housed at the Newberry Library, Chicago, Illinois.

Works Cited

Adair, James. 1974. *Adair's History of the American Indians*. Edited under the auspices of the National Society of the Colonial Dames of America, in Tennessee, by Samuel Cole Williams. New York: Promontory Press.

Allen, David E., and Gabrielle Hatfield. 2004. *Medicinal Plants in Folk Tradition: An Ethnobotany of Britain & Ireland*. Portland: Timber Press.

Anderson, William L. 1984. "Palisot De Beauvois and Cherokee Snakebite Remedy." *Journal of Cherokee Studies* 9(1): 4-9.

Banks, William H., Jr., and Steve Kemp. 2004. *Plants of the Cherokee: Medicinal, Edible, and Useful Plants of the Eastern Cherokee Indians*. Gatlinburg, TN: Great Smoky Mountains Association.

Cozzo, David N. 2007. "The Humors in the Cherokee Ethnomedical System." *Journal of Cherokee Studies* 25:18-42.

———. 2004. "Ethnobotanical Classification System and Medical Ethnobotany of the Eastern Band of the Cherokee Indians." PhD diss., University of Georgia, Athens.

Crellin, John K., and Jane Philpott. 1990. *A Reference Guide to Medicinal Plants: Herbal Medicine Past and Present*. Durham: Duke University Press.

Duke, James A. 1992. *Handbook of Edible Weeds*. Boca Raton: CRC Press.

Fradkin, Arlene. 1990. *Cherokee Folk Zoology: The Animal World of a Native People, 1700-1838*. New York: Garland Publishing.

Fogelson, Raymond D. 1982. "Person, Self, and Identity: Some Anthropological Retrospects, Circumspects, and Prospects." In *Psychosocial Theories of the Self*, edited by Benjamin Lee, 67-109. New York: Plenum Press.

Haley, D. E., F. D. Gardner, and R. T. Whitney. 1924. "Nicotiana Rustica as a Source of Nicotine for Insect Control." *Science* 50(1555): 365-66.

Hamel, Paul D., and Mary U. Chiltoskey. 1995. *Cherokee Plants: Their Uses—A 400 Year History*. Self-published.

Herrick, James W. 1995. *Iroquois Medical Botany*. Syracuse: Syracuse University Press.

Hoffman, Bernard G. 1964. "John Clayton's 1687 Account of the Medicinal Practices of the Virginia Indians." *Ethnohistory* 11(1): 1-40.

Houghton, Peter J., and Ibironke M. Osibogun. 1993. "Flowering Plants Used Against Snakebite." *Journal of Ethnopharmacology* 39:1-29.

Idris, A. M., S. O. Ibrahim, E. N. Vasstrand, A. C. Johannessen, J. R. Lillehaug, B. Magnusson, M. Wallstrom, J. M. Hirsch, and R. Nilsen. 1998. "The Swedish Snus and Sudanese Toombak: Are They Different?" *Oral Oncology* 34:558-66.

Koh, D. C. I., A. Armugam, and K. Jeyaseelan. 2006. "Snakebite Venom Components and Their Applications in Medicine." *Cellular and Molecular Life Sciences* 63:3030-41.

Mahoney, James W. 1857. *The Cherokee Physician or Indian Guide to Health: As Given by Richard Foreman, A Cherokee Doctor*. New York: James M. Edney.

Merrill, William L., and Christian F. Feest. 1975. "An Exchange of Botanical Information in the Early Contact Situation: Wisakon of the Southeastern Algonquians." *Economic Botany* 29:171-84.

Moerman, Daniel E. 1998. *Native American Ethnobotany*. Portland: Timber Press.

Mooney, James. 1900. "Myths of the Cherokee." In *Nineteenth Annual Report of the Bureau of American Ethnology, 1897-98*. Washington DC: Government Printing Office.

———. 1891. "The Sacred Formulas of the Cherokees." In *Seventh Annual Report of the Bureau of Ethnology*. Washington DC: Government Printing Office.

———, and Frans Olbrechts. 1932. "The Swimmer Manuscript: Cherokee Sacred Formulas and Medicinal Prescriptions." *US Bureau of American Ethnology*, Bulletin 99.

Panter, K. E., and L. F. James. 1990. "Natural Plant Toxicants in Milk: A Review." *Journal of Animal Science* 68:892-904.

Payne, John Howard. n.d. *John Howard Payne Papers*. Housed at the Newberry Library, Chicago, Illinois.

PDR (Physicians' Desk Reference). 2004. *Physicians' Desk Reference for Herbal Medicines, 3rd ed.* Montvale, NJ: Thomson PDR.

Radford, Albert E., Harry E. Ahles, and C. Ritchie Bell. 1968. *Manual of the Vascular Flora of the Carolinas.* Chapel Hill: University of North Carolina Press.

Smith, Richard N. 1998. *Wildflowers of the Southern Mountains.* Knoxville: University of Tennessee Press.

Westbrooks, Randy G., and James W. Preacher. 1986. *Poisonous Plants of Eastern North America.* Columbia: University of South Carolina Press.

Witthoft, John. 1984. "Cherokee Beliefs Concerning Death." *Journal of Cherokee Studies* 8(2): 68-72.

Fair Fare?: Food as Contested Terrain in US Prisons and Jails

Avi Brisman

"The degree of civilization of a society is revealed by entering its prisons."
    – Fyodor Dostoyevsky[1]

"No one truly knows a nation until one has been inside its jails."
    – Nelson Mandela[2]

I. Introduction

Prisons and jails, by their very nature, implicate power relations.[3] Although attitudes toward conditions of confinement, as well as the conditions themselves, have changed over the years (evolved or devolved, depending on one's perspective) and may differ depending on the nature of one's offense, incarceration represents an exercise of power (by the State via its agents—prison wardens, prison officials, and correctional guards) over an individual (who has illegally exercised power over another).[4] As Sykes (1958) writes, "The prisoner's loss of liberty is a double one—first, by confinement to the institution and second, by confinement within the institution." Similarly, Catrin Smith (2002, 210) explains: "Imprisonment, in a particularly acute way, challenges a person's autonomy, privacy, control and bodily integrity." Regardless of whether the imprisonment is correct as a matter of fact, or as a matter of law, the prisoner may, in turn, attempt to resist or rebel against this display of power in a variety of legal and illegal, overt and covert, ways.[5]

Despite such efforts at resistance, power relations in carceral institutions may seem like fairly straightforward and imbalanced affairs. But Wolf's (1990, 590) observation that "power balances always shift and change, its work is never done; it operates against entropy" is as applicable inside the prison walls as outside. This paper endeavors to show that not only are power relations in prisons dynamic and complex, but that the very notion of prison as a unitary institution is problematic. Using food as a lens, this paper examines prison power nexuses and contemplates the ways in which prisons are produced by mundane, daily practices and activities and shaped by processes of negotiation, contestation, and variation. The focus is decidedly on US prisons, but examples are also offered from Great Britain, Canada, the Congo, Iraq, Israel, Sierra Leone, South Africa, Turkey, and Uganda.

Part II of this paper begins with a discussion of why food serves as a useful heuristic device for examining dimensions of power in prison. From there, the discussion turns to ways in which the State exercises power over inmates with respect to food practices, including (1) when meals are served, (2) where meals are served, (3) types of food available, and (4) quantity of food.

In Part III, this paper contemplates a five-pronged taxonomy of food-based inmate resistance, considering the significance and efficacy of these individual and group acts of defiance, as well as the types of responses they elicit. In so doing, it endeavors to expose how these tensions contribute to the reproduction of the prison institution.

Part IV offers instances where food functions as a source of "mutual convenience" (R. Martin 1971, 243)—as a means of facilitating the goals of both the State and the prisoner. It looks first at certain types of food-related employment that can provide prisoners with skills upon reentry, thereby improving inmate morale, reducing recidivism, and affecting the public's conception of offenders and ex-offenders. Next, Part IV considers ways in which prisons can positively affect the overall health and nutrition of inmates, thereby benefiting the inmates themselves, their families, and public health in general. Here, food becomes less central and functions as a component of salubrious living and well-being.

Part V concludes with suggestions for further research and study.

II. State Exercises of Power Over Prisoners: Depriving Inmates of Choice

Food is a particularly useful tool with which to investigate power relations in prison because "notions of the body, hunger, food, and power are all closely associated with one another" (Godderis 2006 266n2). Although "food and eating practices have, in recent years, become central to concerns in western societies about the body, health and risk" (C. Smith 2002, 199), the relationship of food to power is not a new phenomenon. For example, the Boston Tea Party (December 16, 1773)—in which American colonists destroyed crates of British East India Company tea to protest British decisions to tax the colonies despite a lack of representation in the Westminster Parliament—and the Tea Act—which allowed the East India Company to undercut the prices of colonial tea merchants—sparked the American Revolution.[6]

The Book of Genesis, to offer another example, describes how God explicitly forbade Adam (and by extension, Eve) to eat from the Tree of Knowledge (2:17); when Eve, and then Adam, ate the forbidden fruit from the Tree of Knowledge (3:6) after being tempted by a serpent (3:1–5), they became aware of their nakedness (3:7) and were banished from the garden, forced to survive through agriculture "by the sweat of [their] face," and made unable to eat from the Tree of Life and live forever (3:19-24). While eating from the Tree of

Knowledge may have resulted in humans having to toil and sweat in the fields, not all sweat and strain has been rewarded equally. Today, farmers in developing countries—most of whom work tiny plots of land without much modern technology, and certainly without satellite imagery to mete out fertilizer—compete with farmers in far wealthier developed countries, whose products are heavily subsidized by their governments. In theory, developing countries should have an advantage in agriculture because of low production, land, and labor costs. But agricultural subsidies allow farmers in developed countries to export their crops cheaply—often for less than it costs to grow them—depriving developing countries of the ability to export crops (Rosenberg 2003; Becker and Thompson 2003; Editorial 2007). At least one commentator has suggested that if the United States ended subsidies for agribusiness, it could reduce immigration by Mexican farmers fleeing the countryside for US cities—"far more effective than beefing up the border patrol"—another issue and locus of conflict and struggle (Rosenberg 2003, A22).

Understanding the prominent emblematic cross-cultural role of food can further illuminate its utility in the exploration of power relations in prison. Morse (1994, 95), for example, contends that food is "the liminal organic substance at the boundary between life and death, need and pleasure; it is also the symbolic medium par excellence." Visser (1991) argues that individuals develop habits of eating certain culturally specific foods in childhood and that the desire to eat these foods becomes an important and powerful form of identity. Similarly, Lupton (1996) maintains that food and eating are fundamental to our sense of self and our experience of embodiment. Likewise, C. Smith (2002, 201-2) asserts that "food, eating habits and preferences are not simply matters of 're-fueling' or alleviating hunger pangs. For most of us, mealtimes represent a break in the day, often a period of sociability. Occasionally, meals are looked forward to as opportunities to (over-)indulge ourselves. Eating habits also serve to mark boundaries between cultures and religions, to distinguish rituals, traditions and festivals, as well as times of the day." Godderis (2006, 255) adds that "eating is not something that just happens to us; on the contrary, all of us 'do' food in some way or another.... The foods we eat, how and where we eat them, and under what circumstances we consume are based on a political, cultural, and familial heritage that extends far beyond our biological need for fuel." And Mintz (1985, 5) proffers:

> Our awareness that food and eating are foci of habit, taste, and deep feeling, must be as old as those occasions in the history of our species when human beings first saw other humans eating unfamiliar foods. Like languages and all other socially-acquired group habits, food systems dramatically demonstrate the infraspecific variability of humankind. It is almost too obvious to dwell on: humans make food out of just about everything; different groups eat different foods and in different ways; all feel strongly about what they do eat and don't eat, and about the ways they do so. . . . [Human beings'] food preferences are close to the center of their self-definition: people who eat strikingly different foods or similar foods in different ways are thought to be strikingly different, sometimes even less human.[7]

These broad comments about food and power provide a backdrop considering how food in prison has been a source of conflict—first as a device of oppression or control, and then (in Part III) as a means of or grounds for rebellion and revolt.[8] In the world outside the prison walls, many of us take for granted the opportunity to choose when (both time and frequency), how much, with whom, and what we eat. Where we select to eat may implicate further choices, such as how we eat (e.g., pizza with our hands, Asian food with chop sticks), and even what we wear while we eat (e.g., shorts and a ball cap to a summer barbeque, a coat and tie to restaurants with dress codes). People with culinary proclivities (regardless of skill) enjoy experimenting in the kitchen and serving their creations to friends and family. Many cooks with such tendencies, as well as many without, take pleasure in varying their diets. Some individuals, for religious or health-related reasons, require certain foods or specific types of food preparation and refrain from certain others. When we lack control over these choices, or when our preferences are ignored, we may become frustrated, angry, or hostile. Almost everyone has encountered an unpleasantly long wait at a restaurant, serving sizes that were too small or too large, and painful meals with in-laws or other dining companions.

Inside the prison walls, food functions "as a symbol of the complexity of power relations between inmates and staff, and between individuals and groups of inmates in this segregated institutional environment" (Valentine and Longstaff 1998, 132). Godderis (2006, 256) writes that "manifestations of institutional power and prisoner insubordination are multi-dimensional and operate on a variety of interacting levels that influence one another.... Food inside prison is one of these elements that acts as a site of contention where struggles over power, and identity (de)construction and maintenance can be played out.... Because of the symbolic power that food possesses, it is a form of communication through which expressions of domination and resistance can be made."

More specifically, the State exercises food-related control over prisoners by depriving them of choice (cf. Valentine and Longstaff 1998, 146). C. Smith (2002, 202) is instructive on this point: "In prison food assume[s] enormous importance, symbolically representing, in many respects, the prison experience. In outside society, dietary habits serve to establish and symbolize control over one's body. In prison, that control is taken away, as the prisoner and their [sic] body become the objects of external forces. Eating choices and preferences are restricted, and the bodily experience of eating becomes mediated and controlled." Indeed, inmates experience little variety in the types of food and meals they receive, and in how the meals are prepared; they possess little autonomy over when, where and with whom they can eat and how long they can take for their meals. They are frequently subjected to rules regarding how they must be dressed when they eat (Foucault 1977, 236; Valentine and Longstaff 1998; C. Smith 2002; Godderis 2006; Blumenthal 2007).[9] But as the following examples illustrate, this power over choice is measured. While possessing the capacity for complete control, the State rarely exercises it, neither repressing to the point of fomenting rebellion, nor offering too many glimpses of freedom that could undercut discipline. Rather, the power exercised is delicately balanced to ensure submission and docility.

When Meals are Served

With respect to when meals are served, Valentine and Longstaff (1998, 137) discuss how the timing of meals in the British male prison that they studied acts as an instrument of control over inmates: "Food is a basic raw material of the body. Through the meal system, the prison regime can therefore literally be inscribed upon the bodies of the inmates. The timing of the meals—inmates are fed earlier than most of them would choose to eat on the 'outside', at 8-8:30 am, 12-12:30, 4-4:30—alters the men's body clocks. There is a sixteen-hour gap between dinner and breakfast, so new inmates must learn to eat when they are not hungry in the morning and afternoon and to control or suppress their bodies' demands for food during the evening."[10] This spacing of meals allows prisons to use food for dual purposes—as something that inmates intensely crave (i.e., in the morning) and something that they might wish to reject but know they cannot (i.e., lunch, served only a few hours after breakfast, and dinner served only a few hours after lunch). Inmates must thus endure the physical discomfort of eating or not eating when they would prefer the opposite, as well as the psychological pain of losing the ability to choose when to eat.

Where Meals are Served/With Whom Inmates May Eat

While prisons and jails differ with respect to where and with whom inmates can eat, all possess some rules relating to these matters. For example, Jose Padilla, the enemy combatant the Bush Administration had accused of plotting a dirty bomb attack and had detained without charges,[11] receives his meals in a slot in a door of his cell (Sontag 2006). Camp 6, the new detention facility in Guantanamo Bay, Cuba, was built with stainless steel picnic tables where detainees were supposed to be able to share their meals. Attacks on guards and inmate suicides have led authorities to clamp down, however, meaning inmates will not be sharing their meals with each other (Golden 2006). In comparison, California law provides that "inmates shall not remove any food from the dining room, kitchen, or food storage areas except as specifically authorized by facility staff" (15 CA ADC § 3055). But in the British male prison that Valentine and Longstaff (1998) studied, inmates spend most of their time locked in their cells. Meals are served from trolleys, with the inmates collecting their food and taking it back to their cells to eat with their cellmates. Although many inmates regard meals as an important break in the boredom of the day and as an opportunity to "create or exploit possibilities to subvert the surveillant gaze of the prison officers," many of them are relieved that they do not have to eat with a large group of prisoners, where tensions can run high and inmates may "beat and bash the shit out of each other for a ladle of milk" (Valentine and Longstaff 1998, 134, 143). The likelihood of violence increases exponentially when dining halls are overcrowded. Wright (1998a) discusses the prison riot that took place on September 26, 1995, at Clallam Bay Corrections Center (CBCC) and reports that the riot stemmed, in part, from the fact that the chow halls could only accommodate approximately ninety prisoners but that guards packed more than twice that number (198 prisoners) into the halls at once. While the actual rules regarding where and with whom inmates eat are prison specific, such rules reflect the broader management role of the prison as well as its goal of punishment through confinement. Not only do rules pertaining to the location of meals reveal the extent to which the prison restricts inmates' abilities to exercise choice, but they underscore the degree to which the prison controls bodily movement.

Types of Food

The US Constitution provides that "Congress shall make no law respecting an establishment of religion, or prohibiting the free exercise thereof."[12] The Supreme Court has held that while "prison walls do not form a barrier separating prison inmates from the protections of the Constitution,"[13] many rights are "subject to substantial restrictions as a result of incarceration."[14] Because "running a prison is an inordinately difficult undertaking that requires expertise, planning, and the commitment of resources,"[15] great deference is granted to prison officials.

Whether inmates are entitled to special meals in accordance with their religious beliefs is a matter with which courts have grappled. For a prison regulation that impinges on inmates' constitutional rights to pass constitutional muster, "there must be a 'valid, rational connection' between the prison regulation and the legitimate governmental interest put forward to justify it."[16] A regulation will not be upheld "where the logical connection between the regulation and the asserted goal is so remote as to render the policy arbitrary or irrational."[17] Courts weigh three additional factors to determine whether a prison regulation that interferes with an inmate's free exercise of religion is reasonably related to legitimate penological interests: (1) "whether there are alternative means of exercising the right that remain open to prison inmates"[18]; (2) "the impact accommodation of the asserted constitutional right will have on guards and other inmates, and on the allocation of prison resources generally. In the necessarily closed environment of the correctional institution, few changes will have no ramifications on the liberty of others or on the use of the prison's limited resources for preserving institutional order. When accommodation of an asserted right will have a significant 'ripple effect' on fellow inmates or on prison staff, courts should be particularly deferential to the informed discretion of corrections officials"[19]; and (3) the absence of ready alternatives as evidence of the reasonableness of a prison regulation; "the existence of obvious, easy alternatives may be evidence that the regulation is not reasonable."[20]

Applying these standards, the US Court of Appeals for the Third Circuit in DeHart v. Horn reversed a decision by the US District Court for the Western District of Pennsylvania, which had found that the refusal by the Pennsylvania State Correctional Institute (SCI) at Greene to accommodate a Buddhist inmate's request for a special diet did not violate his free exercise of rights.[21] The Third Circuit determined that the penological interest in simplified and efficient food service and the avoidance of resentment and jealousy on the part of other inmates constituted legitimate penological concerns under Turner.[22]

Next, the DeHart court concluded that the inmate possessed some alternative means for expressing his Buddhist beliefs. He was afforded other opportunities for religious expression, including prayer, recitation of Sutras, meditation, correspondence with practicing Buddhists, and the opportunity to wear canvas, as opposed to leather sneakers.[23] The fact that vegetarianism is neither a central part of Buddhism nor a commandment of that religion[24] further contributed to the Third Circuit's deciding against an impingement of the inmate's rights under this prong. But noting that DeHart could receive individually prepared foods under an existing administrative process at the SCI at Greene and that inmates at other correctional institutions are served kosher meals would appear to impose a greater burden on prison efficiency and to bring about a similar risk of jealousy, the Third Circuit reversed and remanded the case.[25]

In Williams v. Morton, another Third Circuit case, more than two hundred Muslim inmates at the New Jersey State Prison (NJSP) claimed that prison officials violated their constitutional rights under the Free Exercise Clause of the First Amendment by failing to provide them with Halal meat meals in conformity with their religious beliefs and their equal protection rights under the Fourteenth Amendment, and by providing Kosher meals with meat to four Jewish prisoners, without providing Halal meat to Muslim inmates.[26] In ruling against the Muslim inmates, the Third Circuit held that: (1) the NJSP's decision to provide a vegetarian meal, rather than one with Halal meat, was rationally related to the legitimate penological interests of simplified food service, prison security, and budgetary constraints[27]; (2) the Muslim prisoners possessed other means of religious expression, including a weekly congregational prayer service (known as the *Jumu'ah*); the opportunity to study Arabic and to observe Ramadan by providing a special meal enabling Muslims to comply with the holiday's fasting requirement; the opportunity to pray five times during each day, and the chance to observe the five pillars of the Islam faith; the chance to celebrate Eid—another Muslim holiday, by allowing them to cook their own meals containing

Halal meat[28]; (3) providing Halal meals with meat to such a large population would impose budgetary burdens, create additional security concerns, and cause a considerable disruption to the prison's daily operation in ways that the prison does not experience by providing Kosher meals to only a handful of inmates[29]; and 4) the NJSP could not accommodate the Muslim prisoners' request for Halal meat meals at a *de minimis cost*.[30] Finally, with respect to the Muslim inmates' Equal Protection claim, the Third Circuit held that there was no evidence that Jewish prisoners received meat in their Kosher meals, that all inmates in need of a religious diet are provided vegetarian meals, and thus the prison did not treat Jewish and Muslim prisoners in a "disparate and unequal" manner.[31]

While such holdings indicate that prisons and jails are not required to serve inmates special meals in accordance with their religious beliefs, a number of states attempt to do so. Under Nebraska law, "provisions shall be made for special diets required by an inmate's religious beliefs where reasonably possible" (81 NE ADC Ch. 11, § 006). Similarly, California law provides that "each institution shall make reasonable efforts … to accommodate those inmates who … require a religious diet" (15 CA ADC § 3054[a]). Unlike Nebraska, California takes matters a step further, requiring each correctional institution to provide religious awareness training for custody and food service staff (15 CA ADC § 3054[b]), and specific training for those involved in the supervising, ordering, preparation, and serving of kosher meals (15 CA ADC § 3054.2[f]). Jewish inmates incarcerated at an institution that does not provide kosher meals may be considered for transfer to another institution that can provide the Jewish inmate with a kosher diet, provided that the classification of the receiving institution is appropriate (15 CA ADC § 3054.2[b]). In addition, religious groups are permitted two events per year where foods with religious significance are provided by the institution in place of the regularly planned meal (15 CA ADC § 3053[a]), with Passover constituting a single religious event (15 CA ADC § 3054.2[e]). Finally, where food contains pork or pork derivatives, institutions must identify such foods on the menu with a "P" and offer pork-free alternatives to those inmates who do not eat pork because of religious concerns (15 CA ADC § 3051).

Although adhering to religious dietary customs and eating religiously significant food can help inmates maintain some of their (cultural) identities and connection with their pre-incarceration selves, inmates encounter difficulties accessing ethnic nonreligious dishes (Godderis 2006, 258). Valentine and Longstaff (1998, 136) discuss how the refusal to serve certain ethnic foods helps create disciplined and "docile" bodies: "By embodying a 'traditional' English identity, the prison meals represent one example of a process of *Othering*, marking those who do not share a taste for this food as 'different', in which difference is constructed as negative and inferior. Thus the meals provide a vehicle for prison officers and inmates to articulate disparaging, often racist comments, towards those who express a preference for other types of food, while also denying these inmates the opportunity to express their own identities through the food they consume" (Said 1986). Not only may this result in disciplined or "docile" bodies, but the removal or blockage of positively valued stimuli (i.e., ethnic foods) and the presentation of noxious stimuli (i.e., negative or hostile relations with disparaging and racist guards) may create strain for the inmates and lead to aggression and violence (e.g., Agnew 1992, 2006).

Many prisons and jails in the United States and Britain further remove inmates' capacity for food choice by prohibiting friends and family of inmates from bringing food to the people they are visiting (usually for fear of breach of security and food poisoning),[32] while subsequently placing financial burdens on visitors to purchase "exorbitantly overpriced" food from prison vending machines (Shafer 1991; Grinstead et al. 2001, 67; Domanick 2004, 232; Tewksbury and DeMichele 2005, 305).[33] This impedes prisoners' ability to maintain their cultural identities and connections with the world outside the prison walls, leaves inmates without an occasional dose of variety, and renders them completely dependent on food provided by the prison (Valentine and Longstaff 1998, 134; Eves and Gesh 2003, 168). Hot pots (hot plates) and stingers (immersion heaters used for boiling water) afford some prison inmates the opportunity to exercise a modicum of control over their food intake, but inmates are limited by the foodstuffs offered by the prison commissary—options that may be reduced at any time—and may have their hot pots and stingers confiscated with little or no warning and without recourse (Stough and Pens 1998). However, completely removing choice by closing the commissary or canteen, as it is referred to in British prisons, would be counterproductive. As Valentine and Longstaff (1998, 140) explain, "To the prison officers the canteen is a means to keep inmates docile. They dare not suspend it for fear of inciting trouble."

One of the few instances in which prisoners can select what they eat is when they are on death row and are afforded the opportunity to pick their last meal.[34] But even the last meal is subject to carceral control. Price (2004, 2005), who cooked over two hundred last meals while serving a sentence for sexual assault at the Walls Unit in Hunstville, Texas, explains that condemned inmates often receive something other than what they requested, especially if there are less expensive or more accessible alternatives.[35] Texas Department of Corrections policy provides that only food items kept on hand in the Walls Unit kitchen commissary and butcher shop can be used, meaning that a condemned inmate requesting lobster would receive a filet of processed fish. Lawrence Buxton, executed in February 1991, and for whom Price (2004) cooked his first last meal, received a T-bone steak in place of his requested filet mignon. In 1998, David Allen Castillo requested twenty-four soft shell tacos, six tostadas, two whole onions, five jalapenos, two cheeseburgers, one chocolate milk shake, one quart of milk, and one pack of Marlboro cigarettes. He received four hard shell tacos, six enchiladas, two tostadas, two whole onions, five jalapenos, one chocolate milk shake, and one quart of milk.[36] Despite the discrepancies between what an inmate might request and what he might receive, in Texas, at least, last meal requests are released to the media exactly the way the State receives them (Price 2004).[37] This simultaneously distorts the notion that condemned prisoners receive some comfort during their last hours and revives the "spectacle of public punishment" that Foucault (1977, 9) claims has disappeared.[38]

This, of course, speaks nothing to the issue of quality. While Nebraska law mandates that meals "be prepared with consideration for food flavor, texture, temperature, appearance, and palatability" (81 NE ADC Ch. 11, § 003) and California clarifies sanitation standards (15 CA ADC § 3052), the reality is that complaints of rotten, moldy, or contaminated food are as common in Arizona as in Kurdish prisons in Iraq ("Sheriff" 2003; Sifakis 2003, 123; Chivers 2006).

In apartheid South Africa, the quality of food was linked to race, with white prisoners receiving more nutritious and better-quality food than black prisoners. According to Masha (2004):

> In the food area, where prisoners collected their food from trolleys before moving off to eat in the yard or cells, food drums display the ghastly menu selections prisoners were faced with. African National Congress stalwart Joe Slovo describes the motive for the drums in his unfinished autobiography: "The first drum, marked 'Congress One', contained cooked chunks of beef or pork for white accused. The 'Congress Two' drum, for coloureds

and Indian prisoners, contained either porridge or boiled vegetables on top of which floated a few pieces of fatty meat that were most probably from the discarded cut-offs from 'Congress One' drum. The 'Congress Three' drum (for black prisoners) was always meatless and the contents alternated between a plastic-textured porridge and a mixture of boiled mealies and beans."

In the United States, under the mid-nineteenth-century reign of Elam Lynds, known as the "Whip of Sing Sing," inmates of this Upstate New York prison purportedly received food unfit for pigs. According to Sifakis (2003, 152), "Garbage swill from the convicts' food that was sold to pig farmers proved inferior. The problem was solved by dumping half of the prisoners' rations directly into the garbage so that it would be good enough for pigs. The inmates were simply given less to eat themselves." In 2000, inmates of the US Penitentiary Administrative Maximum Facility (ADX) in Florence, Colorado—a supermax prison that houses some of the most notorious US prisoners, including Theodore Kaczynski (the "Unabomber"), Zacarias Moussaoui (September 11, 2001, conspirator), Terry Nichols (Oklahoma City bombing conspirator), Richard Reid (the "Shoe Bomber"), Eric Rudolph (Olympic Park bomber), and Ramzi Ahmed Yousef (1993 World Trade Center bombing mastermind)—alleged that guards had mixed waste into inmate food (Sifakis 2003, 250). Pens (1995-96) reports claims by Texas prisoners that VitaPro—a soy-based meat substitute—tasted like dog food and caused diarrhea, skin rashes, and other ailments. In 2004, fecal coliform and E. coli were found in the water system at the McNeil Island Correction Center (MICC) near Steilacoom, Washington; E. coli was also found in about 6,000 pounds of ground beef produced at a meat processing plant on the Island prison (R. Smith 2005). Some examples to the contrary exist. I recall meeting an ex-offender—a huge individual nicknamed

"Steroids," about ten years out on parole for assaulting four police officers—who spoke highly of his prison dining experience. "They feed you good in prison," he told me one day. But the overwhelming majority of current and former prisoners consider the food to be poor, with some regarding the low quality as punitive. As C. Smith (2002, 204) recounts, "at the end of the day, steak or Spam, prison food is prison food."

Despite instances of contaminated prison food and negative sentiments about its quality, for many inmates, the issue is not so much actual food, but again, the lack of power and control (Foucault 1977, 236; Valentine and Longstaff 1998, 135; C. Smith 2002). For the female British inmates who served as the subject of Smith's (2002) study, "Food thus becomes symbolic of the fact that life has become restricted and previous values of independence and individualism combine to heighten the pains of imprisonment.... Prisoners are relegated to a child-like state—told when and what to eat—and food becomes associated with penal authority and denial" (C. Smith 2002, 203, 210). Williams (2002a, 299) echoes this analogy, observing that "the prison authorities dictate when prisoners get up, what they wear, what they eat, where they go, with whom they can and cannot speak, and what they can possess. This loss of control infantilizes and dehumanizes prisoners, and it can cause tremendous stress, anxiety, depression, humiliation, and anger." Similarly, Sykes (1958) states that "the frustration of the prisoner's ability to make choices, and the frequent refusals to provide an explanation for the regulations and commands descending from the bureaucratic staff, involve a profound threat to the prisoner's self-image, because they reduce the prisoner to the weak, helpless, dependent status of childhood." Thus, prison food practices, like so much else about prison life, including bathing and sleeping, function as part of the machinery of control over the minute details of an inmate's daily existence.

The fact that the control is pervasive and constant is key. As R. Martin (1971, 247) concludes, "If power is a property of a specific relation between specific individuals or groups in a specific situation, the frequency of the occurrence of that situation is of crucial importance."[39]

Quantity of food

Although carceral exercises of power over type of food—either by serving food of poor quality or by refusing to accommodate religious dietary requests—may be the most common, or at least, the most publicized form of food-related control in prisons, correctional institutions may also manifest their dominion over inmates through food quantity. During the era of Elam Lynds at Sing Sing, prisoners who had money to pay the warden could enjoy double food rations (Sifakis 2003, 152). Similarly, at California State Prison-Corcoran, inmates have received extra food from guards in return for "checking" (beating and raping) other inmates (Wisely 2003a, 249). And Alcatraz, known in its time for being the harshest federal prison, was also recognized as being the best prison for "eats and smokes"—federal prisoners received 3,100-3,600 calories a day (far in excess of the federal guideline minimum of 2,000 calories per day), as well as three packs of cigarettes per week, and unlimited loose tobacco (Sifakis 2003, 10-11). Such "perks" contributed to an element of docility in the prisoners, and with the liberal smoking program, "cigarettes lost the currency value and bribing power they enjoyed in other prisons" (Sifakis 2003, 11). More often, however, prisons exercise control over inmates with less food, rather than with more.[40]

For example, in March 1554, the Oxford Martyrs, Bishops Hugh Latimer and Nicholas Ridley, and Archbishop Thomas Cranmer, were confined at Oxford in the care of city officials until their executions in October 1555 (Latimer and Ridley) and March 1556 (Cranmer). Hammer (1999) reviewed surviving Oxford bailiffs' accounts for Latimer and Cranmer and found that their diets conformed to the general conventions of the period. While individual tastes and situations were accommodated (Hammer 1999, 657-58) and variations in meals served related to both natural seasons and liturgical seasons, with religious influences possessing greater influence than seasonal dietary ones (Hammer 1999, 677), both Cranmer and Latimer ate at a dietary level significantly below that authorized for persons of their status, and Cranmer's precedence as archbishop was not recognized (Hammer 1999, 665).[41] As Hammer (1999, 680) concludes, "In a society as sensitive to small hierarchical distinctions of honor as was Tudor England, there must have been an inescapable sense of meanness about a dietary regime which did not recognize Cranmer's status as an archbishop. Thus, his diet may have incorporated a subtly coded message of humiliation."

To offer a more contemporary example, in the pre-1950s solitary units in Pennsylvania, described as "four-by-four-by-fours" (representing the full dimensions of the cell in feet), prisoners' meals were limited to two slices of bread and water twice a day. Every third day the inmate received a full meal (Sifakis 2003, 111). Today, many states have prison and jail standards for the quantity of food to be served to inmates (Wakeen 2006). Nebraska, for example, requires jail inmates to receive at least three meals per day, one of which shall be hot (81 NE ADC Ch. 11, § 002). In addition, Nebraska jails must meet the dietary allowances as set forth in the Recommended Dietary Allowances, National Academy of Sciences, by serving each inmate the specified serving from each of the five food groups: meat or protein group (two servings per day), milk group (two servings per day), vegetable group (three servings per day), fruit group (two servings per day, both of which could be citrus or tomato juice), and cereal or bread group (three servings per day of whole grain or enriched products) (81 NE ADC Ch.11, § 004). Furthermore, Nebraska law explicitly states that "food shall not be withheld, nor the menu varied, as a disciplinary sanction" (81 NE ADC Ch.11, § 009).

Similarly, California law provides that each inmate shall receive "a wholesome, nutritionally balanced diet. Nutrition levels shall meet the recommended daily allowances established by the Food and Nutrition Board of the National Research Council" (15 CA ADC § 3050[a]). Although California does not codify the number of servings from each food group that an inmate shall receive, it requires that two of inmates' three daily meals be hot (15 CA ADC § 3050[a] 2). But not all states have such regulations, and even in those that do, compliance may fall short. Wright (1998a) discusses assertions by Clallam Bay Corrections Center prisoners regarding reductions in the quantity of food received. Maricopa County (Arizona) Sheriff Joe Arpaio famously cut caloric intake on the nearly nine thousand jail inmates in October 2003 from 3,000 to 2,500 calories per day (Crawford and Scutari 2003; "Sheriff" 2003). Arpaio justified the caloric reduction on health-related and budgetary grounds. "Do you hear me?" he was quoted as telling inmates. "You're too fat. I'm taking away your food because I'm trying to help you. I'm on a diet myself. You eat too much fat" ("Sheriff" 2003). Arguing that he was saving the county about $300,000 a year in food costs, Arpaio boasted: "I got meal costs down to 40 cents a day per inmate. It costs $1.15 to feed the department's dogs" ("Sheriff" 2003).

While Arpaio might wish to further reduce the cost of meals per day per inmate, he would eventually reach a threshold by which the food supplied, or lack thereof, would violate the inmates' rights under the US Constitution. Indeed, with respect to all four categories discussed in this Part—when the meals are served, where the meals are served, types of food available, and quantity of food—there exists a line that the State may not cross without incurring a lawsuit. Thus, to offer an extreme example, the State could not serve all three meals within one hour of each other. Gone, too, are the days of bread and water diets. Thus, while the State possesses the capacity for complete control of inmate food practices—a point noted at the outset of this Part—in this country, it effectively cannot exercise this power because of the rights safeguarded by the Constitution and federal and state statutes. This next Part considers inmate responses to actual and perceived infringement of these rights. In so doing, it alludes to the question of whether the ambiguous location of the line between the State's constitutional exercise of power and unconstitutional encroachment on prisoners' rights actually affords the State greater control than if this boundary were certain.

III. Food-Related Inmate Resistance

Foucault (1978, 86) contends that "power is tolerable only on condition it mask a substantial part of itself. Its success is proportional to its ability to hide its own mechanisms." Foucault maintains that power's success lies in its ability to be anonymous (Rabinow 1984, 19; Garland 1990, 136). In prison, however, power is anything but hidden. The source and mechanisms of power (exercised primarily by the State through wardens, prison officials, and guards, although also manifested by inmate hierarchies) are quite clear. As a result, prison is often intolerable for many individuals. How then does this imbalanced dynamic persist?

Foucault discusses how the prison has been retained despite its failures (Foucault 1977, 271-72; Garland 1990, 149). While this explanation may be useful in understanding why the State has not replaced it with something else, it does not explain why prisoners infrequently rebel.

For Weber (1947, 152), "Power (*Macht*) is the probability that one actor within a social relationship will be in the position to carry out his own will despite resistance, regardless of the basis on which this probability rests." As Arens and Karp (1989, xiii) describe, Weber's conception of power focuses "primarily on the pursuit of individual rather than collective goals." This is exceptionally true in prison, where inmates lack a sense of "we-ness" (Desjarlais 1996, 887) and adhere to the "inmate code" of "do your own time." As Sykes (1958) explains, "The inmate population is shot through with a variety of ethnic and social cleavages which sharply reduce the possibility of continued mass action called for by an uprising. The inmates lack an ideological commitment transcending their individual differences, and the few riots which do occur, are as likely to collapse from dissension among prisoners as from repression by the custodial force."[42]

Combining these perspectives, one could assert that the prison has been retained by those in power because of its failures and has not been overthrown by its detractors because of a lack of unity. (Foucault might suggest that the lack of unity among prisoners, who overwhelmingly represent lower classes, is another reason why the prison has been retained.) Consider Foucault's discussion of Bentham's Panopticon—the circular prison design that provides correctional officials with complete visibility into every cell, "establishing surveillance as a mechanism of disciplinary power without the aid of any physical instrument other than architecture and geometry" (Valentine and Longstaff 1998, 132). Foucault regards the Panopticon as paradigmatic of disciplinary technology over the body. As R. Martin (1971, 250) describes more generally, "The receivers of power signals may anticipate the exercise of power and act accordingly." While some versions of the Panopticon-like centralized circular prison designs do exist, the goal of the prisoner "becoming his own guardian" (Rabinow 1984, 19) has been achieved not by geometry and architectural design, but by the lack of unity in prison. Prisoners must watch their own backs, leading some commentators to suggest that some inmates, especially vulnerable ones, welcome the Panoptic gaze as a form of protection against inmate assault (Valentine and Longstaff 1998, 146-47).

Correctional officers, in turn, recognize this lack of unity and use it to their advantage. While certainly wary of turning a blind eye to gang-related tensions, they realize that permitting some elements of inmate hierarchies and some degree of illegal activity and avoiding crackdowns aimed at complete control and peace may help prevent collective inmate resentment and cooperation that could threaten the (delicate) balance of power and successful operation of the prison (see Valentine and Longstaff 1998, 148-49).

With this tension in mind, this paper turns to inmate "food-based resistance" and the diversity of ways inmates "locate and create consumptive spaces of resistance within the confines of the institution" (Godderis 2006, 255, 265). Godderis (2006, 259-264) categorizes inmate resistance as either "individual" or "group," and further subdivides these categories into four distinct forms of resistance: (1) individual adaptations and adjustments, (2) individual displays of opposition, (3) legitimate group activities, and (4) illegitimate group activities. This paper employs Godderis' typology but offers additional examples and adds an additional category of resistance. In so doing, it attempts to reveal how the prison as an institutional entity is as varied as the tensions within it.

Individual Adaptations and Adjustments

Inmates exist in a world that is neither entirely solitary nor entirely social. On the one hand, unless the inmate is in solitary confinement, prison is a profoundly social experience, with frequently overcrowded living conditions and virtually no privacy. But on the other hand, inmates must constantly watch their own backs and must do what is in their own self-interest in order to survive. Furthermore, Godderis (2006, 257) notes that "how a prisoner chooses to react to the restrictions and deprivations of institutional life is not only based upon the structure of the institution but also upon his or her own unique character and sense of self." This statement echoes Sykes (1958), who writes that not "all prisoners perceive their captivity in precisely the same way. It might be argued that in reality there are as many prisons as there are prisoners—that each man brings to the custodial institution his own needs and his own background, and each man takes away from the prison his own interpretation of life within the walls." Thus, the "inmate code" of "do your own time" and "every man for himself," coupled with the fact that each prisoner experiences prison differently, underscores the solitary nature of prison.

Even though individuals experience prison in very different ways, Godderis (2006, 259) draws some generalizations about inmate coping techniques and discusses how the prisoners she studied would often employ "cognitive tricks" in order "to prevent the distress that was created by the memory of foods and food-related rituals that they used to engage in." Such tricks included actively avoiding cues, such as coupon books, food flyers, and television commercials, that would remind the inmates of food choices unavailable to them in prison, as well as the freedom to take "a trip to the grocery store and purchase the foods that they crave" (Godderis 2006, 260).

C. Smith (2002, 139), however, draws a somewhat different conclusion, implying that if a prison canteen offers particular foods that hold "autobiographical meanings" for inmates—foods that remind them of family, home, and important occasions in their lives—inmates will purchase them in an effort to recapture aspects of their pre-incarceration selves. But Smith recognizes that the prison canteen can neither completely satisfy their cravings for certain foods nor alleviate their pain and longing for food rituals associated with family and home. As Smith explains, the inability to access desired foods means that "food fantasies are as common as sexual fantasies in prison" (C. Smith 2002, 139).[43] Although some prisoners attempt to eat foods that hold "autobiographical meanings," cooking in one's cell presents a number of challenges. Cells do not contain kitchens, meaning that prisoners must cook the foodstuffs they procure from the canteen with hot pots or stingers. But as Angelo (2003, 36-41) describes, inmates are remarkably resourceful, heating food with toilet paper "bombs" (made by loosely wrapping toilet paper around one's hand 12-15 times and doubling it over), "steamer-cookers" (made using three Tupperware bowls and a stinger), and even using the lighting in their cells to heat up sandwiches.

Employing "cognitive tricks" to adjust to the absence of certain foods, on the one hand, and eating foods that hold "autobiographical meanings," on the other hand, represent adaptations by inmates to the types of food in prison. Inmates must also adjust to the quantity of food they receive. As noted above, inmates in some prisons receive their meals in their cells. According to Angelo (2003, 42, 46), one inmate with a metabolic need for large quantities of dairy products would use extra milk obtained from other inmates and kitchen workers to make cottage cheese and yogurt (because the cells lacked refrigeration to keep the excess milk properly). Another inmate would occasionally drop his tray after receiving it through the slot in his door. The inmate would then pick up the tray, return it to the guard, and receive a second tray. While the guard delivering the food would often respond to the dropped tray with annoyance, the dropping of the tray was never intended as an act of defiance. Rather, the inmate, who would meticulously sweep and wash the floor of his cell —from five to eight times a day—would scoop up the food that had fallen and add it to the portion on his second tray, thus allowing him to eat more of a food that he particularly liked.

One final adaptation bears mention. Art in prison has been touted for its ability to help inmates cope with prison life, overcome deprivation, channel anger in positive ways, reduce stress and violence, alleviate depression, enhance levels of patience, produce a calming effect, increase self-respect and confidence, and provide a form of recreation. Art can also afford inmates a means of reflection, foster their creativity, generate a small source of legitimate income, or serve as a commodity (e.g., portraits and greeting cards) that can be exchanged in the prison economy (Durland 1998; Hillman 2002; Thompson 2002; Williams 2002a, 2002b, 2002c; Angelo 2003; Haskell 2003; Williams and Taylor 2004; Carr 2006; Schrift 2006). In addition, art can help inmates replace the label of "I am a criminal" or "I am a prisoner" with "I am an artist" (Thompson 2002, 49). For Donny Johnson, who has not touched another human being in seventeen years, due to his confinement in an 8-by-12-foot concrete cell in the Security Housing Unit of the Pelican Bay State Prison (California), art serves as a solace; his medium is dye from M&Ms, occasionally mixed with coffee or Kool-Aid to produce different colors (Liptak 2006a, 2006c).

Until recently, Johnson, who paints on postcards, would send his finished works through the mail to family and friends. But after his paintings were exhibited at the YAM Gallery in San Miguel de Allende, Mexico, where twenty of them were sold for $500 a piece, prison officials barred Johnson from sending further works through the mail. They charged that Johnson had engaged in a business, defined as "any revenue-generating or profit-making activity," without the warden's permission. Though the proceeds from the exhibition were donated to the Pelican Bay Prison Project, a nonprofit group that helps the children of prisoners, at the time of this paper, Johnson can no longer send his art to his supporters. Whether prison officials lift the restriction, further curtail his privileges, or even extend his sentence, is still to be determined, as is the possibility that Johnson might bring a legal challenge.

Individual Displays of Opposition

For Godderis (2006, 260), inmates frequently challenge institutional dominance with explicit and visibly defiant behavior toward authorities. Such displays of opposition may be short verbal exchanges between the inmate and a guard and often do not lead to systemic changes. But, she claims, "They provide evidence of prisoners' refusal to just be obedient and their rejection of the process of institutionalisation" (2006, 262). As an example, she describes how prisoners in maximum- and medium-security institutions across Canada are often responsible for preparing the food for both prisoners and staff. "Rumours about the contamination of food demonstrate how prison power dynamics remain in constant flux and how easily power can shift from institutional authorities to prisoners. . . . The idea that prisoners could have been polluting the guards' food created the perception (regardless of the reality) that the prisoners were now in control and able to make decisions about something that was vital to the guards' health and well-being. . . . Ultimately it was the mere potential for contamination that allowed for the reversal of power to occur" (2006, 261).

Other examples abound. Inmates who receive their meals in their cells may attempt to make shanks out of the plastic from the trays (Rhodes 2004, 41). Some prisons attempt to discourage this practice by using a particularly rugged and durable tray called the Tivoli III. But because the tray by itself may be used as a weapon (Valentine and Longstaff 1998, 142), inmates must return their trays after meals. Some inmates, however, may refuse to return their trays to provoke guards into entering their cells (Rhodes 2004, 41). Because a specific protocol must be followed for guards to enter an inmate's cell—usually a team of five or six guards donning full gear (akin to a SWAT team) is required for entry—the simple act of withholding one's tray and inconveniencing the guards serves as a statement. Some inmates have no intention of fighting with guards; they just refuse to return their trays and then, when the guards enter, they become passive and allow the guards to cuff them and take the trays. Other inmates, however, want to fight. They know that physical force will be returned, but they hope that they can get in a blow or two—especially if the guard who provoked them is part of the team entering the cell. As Rhodes (2004, 43) explains, "Both sides [guards and inmates] are compelled to respond to the symbolic as well as the overt content of the gestures of antagonism that gather around their points of contact. The apparently trivial tray—the only thing the prisoner can get his hands on—takes on a charge of defiance." While the refusal to return one's tray may serve as a symbolic act of defiance, there is nothing covert about "sliming," whereby an inmate hurls a mixture of "food waste" (Morse 1994, 110)—urine and feces—at guards. Although inmates hope to hit guards in the face with their excrement, burning their eyes, and may attempt to improve the splatter effect by doctoring their concoctions with eggs (Rhodes 2004, 44), "humiliation is the name of the game and is one of the few ways prisoners have to degrade their keepers" (Sifakis 2003, 238). As Rhodes (2004, 45) explains, "In a world where the head of your bed is next to your toilet, where your toilet paper has to be requested, throwing shit says something."

Legitimate Group Activities
A prison's refusal to serve certain ethnic foods can deny inmates the opportunity to express their identities and cultural heritage through the food they consume, creating additional strain for the inmates. At the Canadian prison where Godderis conducted her research, one

"legitimate" form of resistance entailed "ethnic-based food groups." These food groups—formed with the approval of the prison—would coordinate monthly orders of culturally appropriate foods. Food group members could then "either come together to cook an ethnic meal in the kitchen or prepare the food individually in their own units (unless the authorities deemed that the security risks were too high)" (Godderis 2006, 262). Putting aside the issue as to whether actions undertaken with "approval" may properly be considered "resistance," the likelihood of many ethnic-based food groups forming in US prisons is slim because of budgetary burdens on states with overcrowded facilities, security issues, and concerns over disruption to the prisons' daily operations—points raised by the New Jersey State Prison in response to the request by Muslim inmates for Halal meat meals, discussed above.

By far, the most common form of legitimate resistance is complaints, which C. Smith (2002, 205) describes as "endemic in large institutions such as hospitals, schools, and particularly prisons where such complaints [about food] constitute one (legitimate) means of expressing dissent." Complaints can range from simple verbal expressions of displeasure to written grievances within the prison to food-related prison lawsuits. With the Supreme Court's holding in Cooper v. Pate[44] that prisoners may sue prison officials for violation of constitutional rights under 42 U.S.C. § 1983 (which provides that any person acting under color of state law who deprives another person of rights guaranteed by federal law shall be liable to that person), prisoners have turned to litigation seeking legal remedy for constitutional violations (L. Anderson 2000, xiii-xiv).

Recently, in a case entitled Jones v. Bock, the Supreme Court noted that prisoners' lawsuits account for nearly 10 percent of all civil cases filed in federal court.[45] Not all of these cases concern food (see Anderson 2000, xiv). Nor are all cases meritorious. In fact, the

Jones opinion, authored by Chief Justice Roberts, states that "most of these cases have no merit; many are frivolous." While many of these cases do indeed lack merit and while some do sink to the level of frivolous—a point to which this author can attest, having served as a judicial law clerk for the US District Court for the Southern District of Florida—a significant number do raise serious claims, as asserted by Sifakis (2003, 95-97) and as evidenced, in part, by the discussion of DeHart and Williams above.[46] Resistance, however, need not be measured by successful litigation. While certainly some complaints require court-ordered remedies for constitutional violations, some prisoner-litigants may achieve their desired result simply by filing the case. Even the most frivolous case can inconvenience prison staff, judicial staff, and judges. Indeed, the Prison Litigation Reform Act of 1995 (PLRA)[47]—the subject of the Jones lawsuit—was enacted specifically to respond to the large number of prisoner complaints filed in federal court. Even if his case stands on flimsy ground, an angry inmate with a bone to pick can successfully hamstring a court through the legitimate means of litigation.

Illegitimate Group Activities

While any kind of behavior involving multiple inmates that is "not endorsed, or approved of, by institutional authorities" (Godderis 2006, 263) constitutes "illegal group activities," two practices in particular bear mention: (1) the "bootlegged food market" (Godderis 2006, 253) or "black economy" (Valentine and Longstaff 1998, 142), which includes the sale of food products illegally brought into the prison, as well as food stolen or hoarded from the prison kitchen or canteen, and (2) food-related riots. As noted throughout this paper, prisoners exercise little choice over the types of food they eat—a phenomenon that is exacerbated if the prison prohibits family members and friends from bringing inmates food from outside institutional walls. Prison canteens can offer prisoners some avenues for accessing foods that they crave or associate with home or their cultural heritage. But often, the only way to obtain such items is through the underground prison economy. Those inmates who possess the connections to the outside world and the means to bring such items into the prison illegally (often with the help of guards or staff who receive a "cut" for their efforts) control both admission to the market, the nature of the currency, and the rate of exchange—factors that may be difficult to gauge given that "meanings are transient, with products having different meaningful properties for different owners" (Valentine and Longstaff 1998, 140). Nevertheless, these market conditions influence the extent to which the inmate-merchant—Valentine and Longstaff refer to such individuals as "barons" (1998, 142)—is revered or reviled, and with it, the degree of authority within inmate hierarchies. Those inmates who possess the wealth (in whatever form of currency) to buy in this illegal market can resist or at least circumvent some of the oppressiveness brought about by the prison's control over food-related choice.

Aside from food items unavailable through the prison kitchen or canteen, inmates' "black economy" also includes items that are available through these avenues. Kit Kat chocolate bars, for example, can be purchased at many prison canteens. But because the silver foil in which they are wrapped can be used for taking drugs, the bars are stockpiled and traded at exorbitantly high rates, especially if the limit on the number of bars one can purchase at the commissary is low (Valentine and Longstaff 1998, 140-42). For inmate body builders and those involved in the prison gym culture, protein-rich foods and other dietary supplements are highly desirable. The inmate who can acquire such items, frequently by theft from the kitchen, can secure the good graces and protection of those inmates in need. The inmates who can purchase such items "signal wealth (in terms of accumulation) and social standing (in terms of differentiation)" (Valentine and Longstaff 1998, 141). Finally, fruit bought at the canteen or taken from the mess halls can be illegally turned into alcohol, called "pruno," (Valentine and Longstaff 1998, 140; Angelo 2003, 46), which can be traded, sold, or consumed by the vintner, providing a temporary escape (especially if consumed on a holiday or other celebratory occasion).

To some extent, the underground prison economy could be considered a form of indirect resistance. While multiple inmates take part in this illegal group activity for a variety of reasons (status, wealth, hunger, addiction, psychological escape, cultural and personal identifications with pre-carceral lives), the resistance is directed toward the abstract fact of incarceration and the conditions that accompany it, rather than toward a specific individual (such as the warden) or group of individuals (such as the guards). That prison staff may be complicit in dealing contraband, or may turn a blind eye to these dealings of the inmates, underscores the extent to which some people may view the "bootlegged food market" as harmless and even as a necessary means to reduce inmate frustration at their imprisoned existence. Some correctional officers may regard the underground prison economy as vital to preserving the peace, provided that inmates refrain from or limit their disputes over quality and quantity of food items and rates of exchange and provided that the flow of illegal goods into the prison does not seriously undermine prison security. While possessing the potential to virtually entirely shut down these illegal markets, they abstain from doing so in order to avoid illegal group activity directed at guards and other prison staff.

Despite such efforts, prisoners do occasionally focus their anger and frustration at guards and other prison staff, engaging in a direct form of resistance to prison authority and control. Some riots are planned or coordinated events intended for specific purposes (such as to exact revenge on someone or as a response to changes in prison policy). Far more often, they are impromptu events, such as the famous Super Bowl Sunday Chicken Riot at the Graterford State Prison in Pennsylvania, where inmates attacked some guards and locked them in cells in response to an inmate's unsuccessful effort to bring a plate of chicken back to his cell to eat during the Super Bowl (Sifakis 2003, 248-49). In fact, many riots may not be precipitated by an act or actions of prison employees. As C. Smith (2002, 205) explains:

> Mealtimes in prison can be tense occasions where emotions such as resentment, anger and frustration often find expression. Prisoners may express their feelings by leaving the table, shouting, banging trays, spitting food out, or throwing it at staff. Such outbursts are not just about the food itself (which to the outside observer on the whole seemed to be quite good), but rather are about power and powerlessness. In this context, food acts as a prop to establish [prisoners'] refusal to bow under authority. It becomes one means of countering attempts to dictate how [prisoners] should conduct their bodily activities.

Similarly, Valentine and Longstaff (1998, 145) quote a prisoner who wrote that mealtime "can be a time of tension because people are more likely to express discontents when there are a lot of other prisoners together." And Godderis (2006, 263-64) discusses how sitting in a seat that has been occupied by another prisoner is frequently interpreted as a sign of disrespect that may result in a fight. Given the assertion that "people become easily angered by food-related problems" (Godderis 2006, 264) and the fact that a large number of individuals are confined in the small space of a prison cafeteria—recall

Wright's (1998a) discussion of the prison riot that took place on September 26, 1995, at Clallam Bay Corrections Center (CBCC) stemming from an overcrowded dining facility—the smallest slight between two individuals can quickly escalate into a fight drawing in more and more individuals. Because not all inmates will know what prompted the fight, they may become involved if they think that the fight is geared toward guards, especially if they see them intervene. Other inmates may view the fight between a couple of inmates as an opportunity to assault guards and staff—a greater possibility if the ratio between inmates and staff is significantly disproportional. Recognizing the potential for rioting in the dining halls—Valentine and Longstaff (1998, 142-43) note that the metal trays used for carrying one's food can serve as dangerous weapons—some prisons have undertaken measures to reduce the risk of injury to both inmates and staff. For instance, officials at the Louisiana State Penitentiary, Angola, to mix meal ingredients together and bake them into splatter-proof loaves as a disciplinary and precautionary measure designed to take the fun and danger out of food fights (Chaudhry 1991).

The underground prison economy represents an ongoing, habitual, indirect act of resistance to the fact of incarceration and the conditions brought about as a result. Food-related riots represent infrequent, short-lived, direct acts of resistance with far greater potential to cause injury and death and to temporarily disrupt the power relations between inmates and staff. While both of these illegal group activities involve multiple players, neither really symbolizes conscious collective action on the part of the inmates as an expression of a shared ideological position. The "black economy" frequently serves to satisfy real and perceived physical and emotional needs; riots stem from frustration and uncontrolled anger. As stated by Sykes (1958), ethnic and social cleavages in prison reduce the likelihood of mass action resulting in an effective uprising, and ideological disparities (assuming that prisoners even possess formulated ideologies) rarely transcend individual differences. One type of activity does merit discussion for its potential to serve as an illegal group activity built on common philosophical grounds: hunger strikes. But because individual prisoners can undertake this type of resistance, a new category must be added to Godderis' (2006) typology.

Combined Individual and Group Displays of Opposition: Hunger Strikes

Although the term "hunger strike" may seem self-explanatory, a number of sources provide subtly different definitions worthy of mention. The United States Code of Federal Regulations regarding hunger strikes in federal prisons defines an inmate as being on a hunger strike: (a) "when he or she communicates that fact to staff and is observed by staff to be refraining from eating for a period of time, ordinarily in excess of 72 hours," or (b) "when staff observe the inmate to be refraining from eating for a period in excess of 72 hours" (28 C.F.R. § 549.61). Oguz and Miles (2005, 169) describe a "hunger strike" as "an action in which a person or persons with decision-making capacity (often, but not always, in prison) refused to ingest vital nourishment until another party accedes to certain specified demands." They describe a "hunger striker" as "a mentally competent person who has indicated that he has decided to embark on a hunger strike and has refused to take food and/or fluids for a significant interval." For them, two key elements constitute a hunger strike: "the fasting and the statement by the striker to another party that the striker will refuse some or all forms of nourishment or hydration until a specific condition is met" (Oguz and Miles 2005, 169). They further explain that hunger strikes do not entail a complete rejection of all food and water and usually "include the ingestion of some water or other liquids, salt, sugar, and vitamin B1 for a certain time without asserting intent to fast to death" (2005, 169).[48]

Many hunger strikes have been undertaken by prisoners in order to protest the conditions of their confinement, to make political statements or to convey a message about a special cause, or to gain public attention for causes or beliefs important to them (Bennett 1983, 1157; Ludwig 1983, 169; Sunshine 1983, 423; Sneed and Stonecipher 1989, 550; C. Smith 2002, 207; Oguz and Miles 2005, 170; Silver 2005, 632). Bennett (1983, 1157n1) classifies hunger strikes according to four overlapping categories: (1) strikes related to frustration, (2) strikes intended to gain attention, (3) strikes used as a bargaining tool and (4) strikes with irrational suicidal aims. C. Smith (2002, 207) acknowledges these categories, but adds that for some inmates, "the struggle with the body becomes . . . symbolic and some women prisoners seek self-control by deliberately attacking their bodies through self-starvation or binge eating" (C. Smith 2002, 207). For Smith, the refusal to eat food is actually akin to excessive eating, as well as to illegal drug use and deliberate self-harm—all serve as a means for the prisoner to exercise an element of control over his or her body in response to the lack of control over so many other aspects of their incarcerated lives.

> When people are living in an environment in which everything else seems out of their control, where the expression of emotions such as anger and frustration carry their own penalties, certain behaviours, including those often considered "risky" or "unhealthy", can be understood as constituting a rational means of release, a way of coping and of holding on to a sense of self. The pleasures and consolations of such behaviours lead to definitions of "what it is to be healthy" that challenge the dominant meanings constructed in health promotional discourse.

> Thus, certain behaviors, such as self-starvation or "comfort eating", or other health-related behaviors such as illegal drug use and deliberate self-harm, may actually be seen—however paradoxically—as health enhancing in this context. (C. Smith 2002, 210)

This notion of using food to effect control over one's corporeal self is echoed by Silver (2005, 632), who writes that "fasting can . . . be the only plausible way for a prisoner to intentionally bring about his or her own death."[49] Smith and Silver's points notwithstanding, the majority of hunger strikes are undertaken as an effort to bring about change—either within the prison, outside of it, or both.

Historically, self-starvation dates back hundreds of years—as a "practice of the self," as well as "a means of constructing subjectivity" (C. Smith 2002, 207). But as a political weapon, the hunger strike is only slightly more than a hundred years old, with the earliest recorded prison hunger strike taking place in tsarist Russia in 1889, when social revolutionary Vera Figner protested against the unfair manner in which the prison director exercised his authority (Bennett 1983, 1157n1). Gandhi was famous for using the hunger strike as a means of calling attention to his campaigns; between 1918 and 1948, he engaged in some fourteen hunger strikes (although most occurred outside the prison context) (Erikson 1969, 351).[50]

Other notable solo fasters include Nelson Mandela, who fasted in opposition to apartheid (Cave 2006, WK4); Nabil Soliman, who prior to his June 2002 deportation to Egypt refused to accept a tray of food from the Immigration and Naturalization Service because he believed doing so would constitute acceptance of his "illegal detention" (Dow 2003, 269); and Saddam Hussein, who fasted four times to protest his trial and the level of security afforded his defense lawyers (Cave 2006, WK4).

More often, politically driven hunger strikes have been undertaken not as individual displays of opposition but as part of a collective effort to protest a situation or event or to bring about some sort of change. For example, on August 27, 1971, Attica prisoners called a hunger strike in honor of George Jackson, the revolutionary prisoner in California, who was murdered by guards during an escape attempt; only thirteen men ate breakfast and only seven ate lunch (Burton-Rose, Pens and Wright 1998, 217). On June 1, 1992, seven hundred of the eight hundred prisoners at the Waupun medium security prison in Wisconsin went on a one-day food strike, boycotting the dining hall. Inmates were protesting a mid-May 1992 rule created by the Wisconsin Department of Corrections restricting the total amount of property that a prisoner could possess to a footlocker measuring 32 x 16 x 16. Although the stated purpose of the rule was to reduce theft and gambling, Lomax (1998, 225), a Wisconsin prisoner, claims it was geared toward jailhouse lawyers and prisoner writers who accumulate books and paperwork.

Outside the United States, on March 1, 1981, Irish Republican Army (IRA) prisoner Bobby Sands initiated a seven-month-long hunger strike protesting the British government's failure to officially recognize them as "prisoners of war" rather than as "criminals" (Silver 2005, 635; Cave 2006, WK4). Sands and his followers ultimately succeeded in being allowed to wear their own clothes and were no longer required to work in prison, but they were never able to regain their desired political status, and ten prisoners, including Sands, eventually starved to death in protest (Silver 2005, 635). In the Middle East, Palestinians have occasionally used hunger strikes to oppose their treatment by their Israeli captors: a starvation campaign in 1980 by Palestinians held in an Israeli prison led to force-feeding and the death of two prisoners (Cave 2006, WK4), and in 2004, three thousand Palestinian inmates from several prisons initiated a hunger strike demanding better conditions in Israeli jails (Silver 2005, 634). At the American military prison at Guantanamo Bay, Cuba, detainees held by the United States have fasted in protest of the conditions and the length of their confinement (Silver 2005, 633; Cave 2006, WK4; Golden 2006, A1, A12).

While virtually every region of the world has now witnessed some individual or group of individuals starving for a cause, two notable examples come from Turkey. From April 25, 1996, until July 27, 1996, 355 Turkish prisoners in forty-three prisons around the country undertook a hunger strike to protest the transfer of political prisoners from Diyarbakir E-Type Prison to Eskisehir Prison, a notorious high-security prison known as "The Coffin" (Benyon 1996, 737). The hunger strikers demanded repeal of the transfer order, an end to the severe beatings during transfers to and from court or hospital, a stop to the policy of sending remand prisoners to prisons far from their families and legal counsel, and a cessation of ill-treatment to relatives who visit political prisoners. In a negotiated settlement, 102 political prisoners who had been transferred to Eskisehir Prison were sent back to prisons in and around Istanbul, but not before twelve prisoners had died and 170 had received medical care. Many of the survivors were left with damaged internal organs, particularly to the brain, as well as metabolic disorders. As Benyon (1996, 737) concludes, "In a state where intimidation, detention, torture, and extra-judicial killings are used to silence dissent, the hunger strike is the prisoners' best hope to focus international attention on human rights abuses in Turkish prisons."

Similarly, in 2001, nationwide prison reforms in Turkey (specifically the replacement of dormitory-style prisons with one- and three-man cells) sparked strikes that lasted for months (Silver 2005,

634-35; Cave 2006, WK4). Scott Anderson (2001, 42-47, 74, 124-25) describes this strike as the longest and deadliest hunger strike against a government in modern history. Aside from the length of the strike and the sheer number of people who died,[51] what makes the 2001 Turkish hunger strike noteworthy is that it was undertaken by a combination of current inmates, former inmates, and individuals outside prison who had no direct connection with the inmates in the new prisons.[52] As Anderson (2001, 42-47, 74, 124-25) explains, many of the strikers outside the prison were young individuals from poor backgrounds with little education and few prospects; striking provided them with a sense of identity and purpose.[53]

Speaking more generally, Anderson (2001, 42-47, 74, 124-25) observes:

> A hunger strike might seem to be an act of ultimate desperation, a weapon of last resort for the powerless, but the reality is a bit more complex. Politically motivated hunger strikes tend to occur in a very specific kind of society and at a very specific time: namely, in places with a long history of official repression, but where that repression has gradually begun to loosen. If it is the institutionalized nature of abuse that fuels the strikers to such extreme action, it is the cracks of liberalization that lead them to believe that such a course might shame the government into change—and often they are right.

Because hunger strikes—"one of the few weapons available to prisoners" (Powell 1983, 714) and "one of the few ways in which a person without access to weapons or poisons can make a life or death decision" (Oguz and Miles 2005, 170)—have proven to be potent tools for effecting change (Ansbacher 1983, 99), they occur frequently. While most are of brief duration, occasionally, as in some of the incidents described above, prisoners have risked or suffered serious health impairment or death from prolonged hunger strikes. In these situations, prison officials have attempted to force-feed inmates.[54]

Force-feeding—essentially, any "undesired artificial feeding" (Ansbacher 1983, 99-100n7)—is generally accomplished using one of the following three methods: (1) nasogastric tube feeding, which is performed by inserting greased tubes through the nose, down the esophagus, and into the stomach, (2) intravenous feeding, which requires the insert of a catheter into a blood vessel that leads to the heart and (3) gastrotomy, which necessitates direct surgical access to the stomach, and is considered an option of last resort (Ansbacher 1983, 124-25; Greenberg 1983, 750; Powell 1983, 725; Sneed and Stonecipher 1989, 553n34; Silver 2005, 637-38). All three methods involve varying degrees of physical intrusion. Gastrotomy, as noted above, is the most intrusive. Intravenous feeding is the least obtrusive of the methods, but it is slow and cannot be performed safely on a struggling prisoner, and thus can be used only on an inmate who is too weak to resist or who has been sedated (Ansbacher 1983, 124; Powell 1983, 730; Sneed and Stonecipher 1989, 553 n.34; Silver 2005, 637-38). Many doctors, on both medical and moral grounds, oppose putting a hunger striker in an artificial unconscious state in order to feed him intravenously (Ansbacher 1983, 124; Powell 1983, 725). In addition, the procedure carries the risk of infection (Silver 2005, 637-38).

In contrast, inserting a nasal gastric tube through the nose and into the stomach is the most commonly employed method, and the one preferred by many prison officials (Ansbacher 1983; Powell 1983, 725; Silver 2005, 637-38). But this method also requires cooperation from the prisoner and may cause pain, illness, or death (Ansbacher 1983, 125; Powell 1983, 730; Silver 2005, 637-38). Even if the prisoner does not resist, the risks are considerable: the tube may choke the patient; its removal often induces vomiting; vomit may enter the lung along with hydrochloric acid attached to the end of the tube from the stomach lining, leading to pneumonia (Ludwig 1983, 172n16).

Because eating is such a normal and necessary activity (see, e.g., Ansbacher 1983, 105), inmates have challenged prison officials' attempts to force-feed them, claiming that they should be allowed to determine for themselves what beliefs are worth dying for (Cantor 1973, 244) and that force-feeding a competent inmate violates that inmate's fundamental privacy rights and rights to autonomy (Sneed and Stonecipher 1989, 553; Silver 2005, 632, 661). Unlike in Great Britain, which has officially recognized a prisoner's legal right to starve (Silver 2005, 635), in the United States, nearly fifteen state and federal courts have declined to recognize a prisoner's right to refuse invasive medical treatment (regardless of the individual's status as a convicted inmate, a pretrial detainee, or a person being held pursuant to a civil contempt order (Silver 2005, 638)). These courts have held that prison officials may force-feed a hunger-striking prisoner despite the health and safety risks involved in the above-mentioned highly invasive methods (Silver 2005, 632). In general, these courts have tended to find that the government's interests in the preservation of life and in maintaining prison security and effective prison administration outweighs prisoners' due process and First Amendment rights (e.g., Bennett 1983, 1230; Sneed and Stonecipher 1989, 561-62; Silver 2005, 661). Or, as one journal claimed in the mid-1970s, "To accede to the prisoners' demands as a result of a hunger strike would establish an altogether too easily invoked Court of Appeal by Hunger, enabling any prisoner with determination and a long sentence who had run the full course of the legal process to reopen his case" ("Force Feeding" 1974).

Given the virtual unanimity on the issue of force-feeding, some authors question whether inmates will continue to rely on hunger strikes as a political weapon. Cave (2006), for example argues that the hunger strike is losing its strength as a political weapon: "Fasting for a cause is less novel, what constitutes a fast is more loosely defined, and the technology of force-feeding has grown less barbarous. ... Like all forms of protest, the hunger strike is only as successful as the protester or cause is sympathetic. The largest obstacle to rallying support for [individuals such as Saddam Hussein] is the man himself." But for others, hunger strikes will continue to play an integral role in prison-based political discourse. As Oguz and Miles (2005, 170) contend, "For prisoners, conventional means of political expression such as voting, donating to political organisations, publishing, or national organising are greatly diminished. They are obstructed, impracticable, or illegal. Under these circumstances, a hunger strike asserting bodily integrity is one of the few tools for strong political expression." Hunger strikes thus play an interesting role in the typology of prison-inmate power relations. Because hunger strikes may be undertaken for a wide range of reasons, including frustration, a desire to gain attention (for a particular cause), or as a bargaining tool, and because an inmate can fast alone, in concert with fellow inmates, or with individuals outside the prison, the hunger strike has varying potential as a challenge to State authority. How the State chooses to respond to the hunger strike affects the strength of this challenge, although as Oguz and Miles (2005, 170) contend, "Any response by the state including neglect, negotiation, or forced feeding is a form of dialogue with the strikers and with the broader audience of the strike." Allowing the hunger striker to die, they continue, "ratifies the charge that the authority does not value the personhood of prisoners." But on the other hand, "forced feeding to 'save life' draws attention to the way the diminished quality of life has inspired the protest" (Oguz and Miles 2005, 170).

The attention that force-feeding may bring to the issue that has engendered the strike may in some ways favor the prisoners in the prison-inmate power seesaw. But it is important to consider that the State's response to this form of prisoner dissent constitutes not only physical intrusion into the inmate's body but also intrusion into the individual's decisionmaking about the self. Regardless of the attention that force-feeding may bring to the inmate's cause, force-feeding still represents a shift in the power relations over the prisoner' body, with the State once again asserting its dominance. The inmate is then left with the option of challenging the force-feeding in court. But this action turns an illegitimate activity—the hunger strike—into a legitimate one—the court challenge to the forced ending of the hunger strike. More significantly, whatever attention might have been paid to the issue that spurred the hunger strike is likely to dissipate—both as a result of the shifted attention to the case, rather than the cause, and because litigation is far more time-consuming, far more abstract, and far less visceral than fasting. The only real hope for the protestors to keep the attention fixed on the cause is if individuals outside the carceral system (who have broader rights than prisoners) fast as well. Not only are such instances rare, but as the fasts continue over days, weeks, and months, and as the number of deaths increases (a situation that occurred with the 2001 hunger strike in Turkey), the focus invariably shifts to the fact of not eating, rather than the reason for it.

In this light, hunger strikes, more so than individual adaptations and adjustments, individual displays of opposition, legitimate group activities, and illegitimate group activities, represent the greatest gamble for the prisoners involved. While the potential payoff is great—attention within and outside of the prison to the inmates' cause, sympathy from the public, embarrassment to the prison, and the success of achieving the desired change(s)—the risk is immense.

Force-feeding, perhaps more so than the examples offered in Part II, intrudes on the body but impounds the soul. Foucault claims that "punishment as a public spectacle of violence against the body" was replaced by punishment "aimed to affect the 'soul' of the offender" (1977, 7-23; Garland 1990, 135-36). Force-feeding may achieve both and, depending on the circumstances, may remove the public spectacle, leaving only the violence against the body and the soul.

IV. Power Relations of Mutual Convenience

For R. Martin (1971, 243), some "power relations may be relations of mutual convenience: power may be a resource facilitating the achievement of the goals of both A and B—in the same way as money may facilitate the achievement of the goals of both borrower and lender in a credit relation." Although power relations in prison typically involve exercises of control (over inmates) and attempts at resistance (by inmates), there are a few instances in which goals of both the prison and the inmates are achieved. This is not to suggest that power is absent on such occasions, nor is this to imply that a measure of equality is achieved. Rather, the following examples represent situations that are beneficial to both the prison and the inmates.

Prison labor usually does not conjure up images of friendly workplaces with employees content with their salaries, benefits, and hours. Foucault (1977, 243) asks, "What, then, is the use of penal labour? Not profit; nor even the formation of a useful skill; but the constitution of a power relation, an empty economic form, a schema of individual submission and of adjustment to a production apparatus." With the growth of the private prison industry, penal labor frequently generates tremendous profits for corporations. At the same time, penal labor allows the State to receive something in return for the expense of feeding, housing, and clothing its prisoners, while also functioning as means of inmate control—"a schema of individual submission" (see, e.g., Wright 1998b, 102-06; Pens 1998c, 107-08; Cahill 1998, 109-11; Cahill and Wright 1995, 112-13; Pens 1998b, 114-21; Levassuer 1998, 122-26; Burton-Rose 1998, 127-31; Wright 2003, 112-19; Lafer 2003, 120-28; Burton-Rose 2003, 129-32; Lomax 2003, 133-35; Sifakis 2003, 294-96; Levister 2006). Although penal farms, which predate private prisons, have a long history of oppression and cruelty (Oshinsky 1997; cf. Inciardi, McBride, and Rivers 1996, 23-24), the insect "farming" program at the Seminole County Correctional Facility in Florida has generated benefits for both the correctional facility and the inmates (Woods 2004, 2005).

At the Seminole County Correctional Facility in Sanford, Florida, where inmates have been growing their own vegetables for over ten years, inmates raise two types of "beneficial bugs"—one that preys on insect pests and another that feeds on troublesome weeds. The insects raised by inmates reduce the need for chemical pesticides and, if the project continues to develop, could save taxpayers money in the fight against new invasive pests. Inmates, on the other hand, receive training and certification from the University of Florida's Institute of Food and Agricultural Sciences, which could help them secure employment upon release from the correctional facility.

In a somewhat similar vein, correctional facilities in Connecticut, Georgia, and Indiana have employed inmates to grind, mix, monitor, and turn nitrogen-rich vegetable scraps from food service programs (Allen 1994; Block 1997; "Waste Wood" 2001). By diverting organic waste from landfills, thereby reducing waste and conserving water, such prison composting programs reduce organic loading (nitrogen and BOD—biochemical [biological] oxygen demand) and produce better landscaping through compost application. Inmates, in turn, learn meaningful skills that they might be able to use upon release. Equally important, if not more so, prison composting has improved public perception of the correctional system (Block 1997), which helps ex-offenders avoid some of the stereotyping, stigmatization, and negative labeling that accompanies a prison record (Livingston 1996; Brisman 2004).

While certain types of food-related prison employment can help meet the goals of both the prison and the inmates, prisons offer the opportunity to positively affect the overall health of inmates. Following through on this opportunity can benefit the inmates (a segment of the population arguably most "at risk" for ill health) and their families (upon the inmates' return to their communities), can relieve burdens on community health care systems, and can save taxpayers money in health-related costs for prisoners and former prisoners (C. Smith 2002, 198). As C. Smith (2002, 198) explains, "Prisoners, on the whole, seem to be a pretty unhealthy lot. There is evidence that the physical and mental health of the prison population is worse than that of the general population." The fact that many prisons offer nutritionally deficient food or foods high in starch and fat content does not currently seem to help matters (Sifakis 2003, 281).[55] Godderis (2006, 258) refers to the "monotonous and repetitive nature of the food served" in the Canadian prisons she studied, adding that inmates were frustrated by their inability to direct how the food was cooked, for example, baking versus deep-frying, which subsequently prevented them from being "in full control of their own health." Likewise, Valentine and Longstaff (1998, 138) have found that the lack of control over how meals are prepared, combined with the lack of exercise as a result of sedentary lifestyles, results in a deterioration of the inmates' bodies in the form of weight gain, a change in the pallor and condition of their skin, constipation, or diarrhea (which is particularly feared because inmates experience shame and embarrassment using the toilet under the surveillant gaze of prison officers).[56] But the potential for promoting healthy eating practices—as part of overall strategies to improve inmates' nutrition and health—exists.

Although prison may be harrowing for men and women alike, regardless of their family situations, "incarceration of pregnant women may emotionally traumatize the women through environmental restrictions, separation from family/friends, and concerns regarding the placement of the expected baby (newborns are usually placed with the women's families soon after delivery)" (S. L. Martin et al. 1997, 1526). Such trauma is often increased through the practice of shackling female prisoners during labor, delivery, and recovery (Editorial 2006; Liptak 2006b). While most pregnant inmates are nonviolent offenders who pose little risk of flight or attack on hospital staff, prison rules are frequently exported to hospital settings, meaning that inmates must deliver their babies (about two thousand babies are born to American prisoners each year) without anesthesia while strapped to delivery tables (Editorial 2006; Liptak 2006b).[57]

Putting aside the issue of shackling and anesthesia, which present risks for both the inmate giving birth and the infant, S. L. Martin et al. (1997, 1531) found that "infants born to women incarcerated during pregnancy were not significantly different from infants born to never-incarcerated women in terms of their birthweights; however, the birthweights of infants born to women incarcerated at a time other than during pregnancy were significantly lower than the birthweights of both infants born to never-incarcerated women and the infants born to women incarcerated during pregnancy." Such findings led the authors to conclude that incarceration may actually enhance the health of some pregnant women and may foster healthy pregnancy outcomes. Although "prison is no panacea for the problems of high-risk pregnant women, including substance-abusing or substance-dependent women. . . . incarceration may improve women's health by supplying these often high-risk women with shelter and regular meals, restricting their alcohol and illicit drug use, limiting physically demanding work, eliminating sexual intercourse with male partners, and eliminating physical/sexual abuse by their male partners. Furthermore, prisons are required to provide all pregnant inmates with appropriate prenatal health care services" (S. L. Martin et al. 1997, 1530-31). While prison health care is often substandard (see, e.g., Cusac 2003; Herivel 2003; Sherwood and Posey 2003; St. Clair 2003: Talvi 2003; Wisely 2003; Young 2003; Pfeiffer 2004; Editorial 2005; von Zielbauer 2005a, 2005b, 2005c; Urbina 2006), for some women, it may be the only prenatal health services they receive. If such health promotion includes nutritional eating practices before delivery and carries on afterward, then health promotion in the prison context should be regarded as a matter of public health, not just prisoners' health. This should hold true for women who are not pregnant as well. As C. Smith (2002, 198) points out, "Women prisoners . . . have been identified as a group for whom health promotion is seen as especially important, not merely for their own benefit but also because of their assumed responsibility for the health of others"—a responsibility that they may be more willing to accept and assume given that for many mothers, "not knowing or having control over the lives of their children is one of the most frustrating parts of being incarcerated" (Williams 2002c, 142).

Whereas a healthy diet in prison may benefit women, regardless of pregnancy, both during incarceration and after (if they continue to eat well) and holds the potential to positively affect their families upon release (if the released women transmit nutritionally responsible eating practices to their families), the impact of a healthy diet in prison for men is somewhat different. For example, Hibbeln, et al. (1998) have found that low concentrations of docosahexaenoic acid, a polyunsaturated omega-3 fatty acid, may increase predisposition to hostility and depression and that abnormalities in essential fatty acid metabolism may be present in violent offenders. Gesch et al (2002), in an experimental, double-blind placebo-controlled, randomized trial of nutritional supplements on 231 young adult prisoners, comparing disciplinary offenses before and during supplementation, found that antisocial behavior in prisons, including violence, is reduced by vitamins, minerals, and essential fatty acids, with similar implications for those eating poor diets outside prison walls. Although Gesch et al. (2002, 26) were careful not to attribute antisocial behavior entirely to nutrition, they asserted that "the difference in outcome between the active and placebo groups could not be explained by ethnic or social factors, as they were controlled for by the randomised design." They concluded that supplementing prisoners' diets with physiological dosages of vitamins, minerals, and essential fatty acids (omega-6 and omega-3, which foster the growth of neurons in the brain's frontal cortex—the portion of the brain that controls impulsive behavior) caused a reduction in antisocial behavior to a remarkable degree. They suggested that further reductions in antisocial behavior could be achieved by providing violent subjects with foods containing proportionally more fatty acids and advocated additional research to understand how food may improve understanding of established risk factors (2002, 26-27).

The "potential implications of diet on behavior" (Eves and Gesch 2003, 168) can be regarded as interesting and exciting from a public health perspective, but intervention in the lives of captive populations raises a number of concerns, especially with respect to the power relationships between prisoners and the State. First, the history of the Tuskegee syphilis study has left many African Americans, who are disproportionately represented in US prisons and jails, with distrust for research and treatment (Washington 2007). Second, prisoners of all ethnicities who do not generally distrust research and treatment and who might actually participate in research outside the prison walls may be unwilling to participate inside the prison as a way of demonstrating and affirming their agency in their sense of capacity to choose. The potential for such a response is particularly great if the foods being introduced do not possess ethnic significance or if the foods being replaced do—"for those who would change . . . eating habits . . . there is always the problem of tradition and identity" (Dewan 2006). In order to prevent inmates from viewing interventions as "culinary hegemony," C. Smith (2002, 199) urges researchers "to consider personal health belief systems and the relative values individuals attribute to health." Third, those who do take part in prison-based research and treatment might associate certain eating practices with prison and find themselves disinclined to continue such practices upon reentry in order to erase painful memories of incarceration, thereby minimizing some of the potential public health gains.[58] Finally, Smith (2002, 199, 211) notes that some inmates may simply not be interested in changing their eating patterns, "It remains a paradox that while people may be well aware that certain behaviours are 'risky' and may lead to illness, disease and even death they continue to engage in them. . . . Knowing that certain behaviours are potentially self-harmful may be considered a precondition for taking them up in the first place and/or maintaining them. . . . The more a behaviour is denounced as unhealthy, the more pleasurable it becomes, especially for those with few alternative avenues of pleasure, such as prisoners."

In addition to the obstacles that researchers may encounter with respect to inmates, the public may also balk at the notion of attempting to change violent behavior through food. As Mihm (2006) contemplates, "What would it mean if we found a clear link between diet and violent behavior? To start with, it might challenge the notion that violence is a product of free will. . . . The belief that people choose to be violent may be irrelevant if the brain isn't firing on all cylinders. This may especially be the case for impulsive acts of violence, which are less a choice than a failure to rein in one's worst instincts." For an example, recall that in the 1979 trial of Dan White for the shooting deaths of San Francisco Mayor George Moscone and Supervisor Harvey Milk, White's counsel offered the "Twinkie Defense," suggesting that junk food was partially to blame for his "diminished capacity" (Fleetwood 1987; Pogash 2003; Dreeben 2006) The jury believed the argument that a poor diet contributed to White's compromised mental state and found him guilty of only voluntary manslaughter. Instead of the death penalty, White received a sentence of fewer than eight years, for which he served five years, one month, and nine days. Although White's allegedly poor diet actually played a minor role in his attorneys' attempt to explain White's depression (Dreeben 2006), the media jumped on the concept of the Twinkie Defense. Outrage in the California state legislature over the White trial led to the abolition of the "diminished capacity" defense, but the term "Twinkie Defense" lives on and is used to describe "a seemingly absurd defense strategy that somehow works" (Dreeben 2006, 348 n.5). That the Twinkie Defense leaves a bad taste in the mouths of many people may serve as an indication of public response to attempts to alter violent behavior through food. As Mihm (2006) contends, "There's something that many people may find unnerving about the idea of curing violent behavior by changing what people eat. It threatens to let criminals evade responsibility for their actions." More controversial, he goes on to suggest, "is the brave-new-world idea of using diet to enforce docility and conformity to the rules, a sort of state-sponsored version of that timeless parental demand to children everywhere: 'Eat your vegetables.'"

Relations of "mutual convenience" may emerge in food-related prison employment and in the promotion of healthy eating practices as part of overall strategies to improve inmates' nutrition and health. But such relations should not be mistaken as devoid of power or as egalitarian. Rather, they simply, temporarily, and in a very limited way, shift the penal system from punitive to corrective—from a system intent upon dispensing punishments to one intent upon "producing normal, conforming individuals" (Garland 1990, 136). As such, they may offer on some levels a qualitatively different prison experience for some inmates, but it is not an experience lacking the processes of negotiation and contestation between prison authorities and prisoners, and between prisoners and each other, that shape the modes and varieties of domination inside the institutional walls.

V. Conclusion: Directions for Future Research

Using food as a domain through which meanings, practice, identities, and relations are defined and contested, this paper has attempted to set forth a conceptual framework with which to understand power dynamics in prison. While the focus has clearly been on the ways in which food mediates power relations within the prison, it speaks to and may be a part of broader issues of power, such as the relationship between the prison and the community in which it is situated and the ways in which prisoners are conceptualized within society. Two potential avenues of future food-based inquiry may help shed light on these broader prison-community and prisoner-society relationships.

First, Block (1997) found that prison composting has improved public perception of the correctional system. Additional research should be conducted to further comprehend the ways in which the relationships between prisons and prison communities and between prisoners and non-prisoners contribute to or decrease power inequalities. Although poor rural communities in cash-strapped states frequently woo private prison companies in the hope of boosting sagging economies (Pens 1998a; Silverstein 1998; Crawford and Scutari 2003; Abramsky 2006), such communities frequently regard prisoners as chattel or commodities and prisons in purely economic terms. While studies should continue to explore these types of relations, research should also examine interactions between prisons and prison communities that may serve to reconceptualize inmates in more positive terms. For example, Brown (2006) discusses the garden operated by the nonprofit Food for Thought organization in Sonoma County, California, that provides fresh produce for people who have HIV or AIDS; she reports that the garden "is part of a broader move to bring organic food and a bit of the wild into places where it has been lacking, among them schools and prisons." Research could examine the circumstances under which organic food is brought into prisons and jails, how this process affects the conceptions of criminals and inmates by those who grow and deliver the food, as well as whether the inmates regard the extramural world and its more conventional values differently as a result of interactions with organic food aficionados.

Second, in the field of criminology, labeling theories posit that arrest, conviction, and imprisonment and the accompanying process of defining the individual as a "criminal," "delinquent," "felon," or "offender" may push that individual toward committing further crimes—essentially a self-fulfilling prophecy. As Livingston (1996, 379) describes, "Other people will respond to the label rather than to other facts about the person, and this response will make it more difficult for the labeled person to move easily into noncriminal society." Zernike (2005), however, examines a situation in which labeling theory does not apply. She reports how the Minnesota Correctional Facility in Shakopee, Minnesota, which lacks a wall or fence separating the facility from the community residents, rents plots of land to local gardeners and allows neighbors to bicycle and jog through the prison grounds. The inmates used to keep a farm where they raised chickens and milked cows, and for a time, they ran a day-care center. Residents of the community have balked at proposals to put a fence around the facility, noting that when inmates come out to play ball, they see neighbors cutting their lawns and performing other tasks involved with home ownership—activities that provide the inmates with positive images of noncriminal lives. Additional research is needed to examine prisons and jails, such as the one in Shakopee, to understand how efforts to break down the literal and figurative walls between prisons and the surrounding communities —how attempts to foster positive relations between prisoners and residents of the communities where prisons are located—can help reduce the labeling effect that frequently comes with the moniker "criminal."

These two inquiries could beget a third. At the outset, this paper noted that "food and eating practices have, in recent years, become central to concerns in western societies about the body, health and risk" (C. Smith 2002, 199). Such heightened concern has led to bans on trans fats and increased attention to where food comes from, as evidenced by the growing popularity of local and organic produce and meats and the emerging consideration of food labor practices. But what is considered to be a healthy diet and responsible eating is frequently determined by the "dominant class" (Bourdieu 2000, 206) and beyond the reach of those with low incomes (C. Smith 2002, 211). As a result, low-income individuals are not only unable to engage in salubrious eating habits, but must suffer the ignominy of eating foods that are neither hip nor healthy.

Bourdieu (2000, 205) asserts that "aversion to different life-styles is perhaps one of the strongest barriers between classes." Research is needed to explore the extent to which power inequalities with respect to food outside prison contribute to or even exacerbate power inequalities inside the prison walls and vice versa, especially given that "lower socio-economic and otherwise marginalised groups are over-represented in the prison population" (C. Smith 2002, 198). A greater understanding of the ways in which attitudes toward food and eating practices permeate prison walls in both directions could shed light on macro-level social interactions and the ways in which other contemporary techniques of power and control operate.

Notes

* Reprinted with minor editorial changes with permission of the publisher, *Georgetown Journal of Poverty Law and Policy* © 2008.

1. Dostoyevsky (1923, 76).

2. Mandela (2000).

3. Although "prisons" refer to state or federal facilities of confinement for convicted criminals, especially felons, and "jails" refer to places where persons awaiting trial or those convicted of misdemeanors are confined, unless otherwise indicated, this paper will use the term "prison" as a shorthand to refer to both types of facilities. Nagin (1998, 1) provides a succinct description of power relations in the criminal justice system: "The criminal justice system threatens punishment to law breakers—through the police power to arrest and investigate, the judicial power to adjudicate and sentence, and the corrections agencies' power to administer punishments."

4. For example, Daly and Wilson (1997, 53) state that "crime consists overwhelmingly of self-interested action conducted in violation (or reckless disregard) of the interests of others." Similarly, Arens and Karp (1989, xv) contend that "power may always involve the exercise of an individual's will over another's, but the rationale and basis for domination, acquiescence, and resistance may vary considerably from one cultural setting to another." And Ferrell (1994, 176) discusses how crime can be an act of political resistance and rebellion in some instances, but that in others, such as with rape, crime perpetuates "violent, hierarchical arrangements."

5. Compare Foucault (1978, 95), who succinctly asserts, "Where there is power, there is resistance," with Abu-Lughod (1990, 42), whose provocative essay posits, "Where there is resistance, there is power."

6. The Boston Tea Party has inspired other acts of resistance and rebellion, including the Indian salt protest campaign (also known as the Salt Satyagraha and the Salt March to Dandi) led by Mahatma Gandhi against the British in 1930 (Erikson 1969, 448).

7. Other examples abound. Valentine and Longstaff (1998, 131-32) provide a representative sample of sources by anthropologists, sociologists, and geographers.

8. For Foucault (1978, 93), this is obvious, as evidenced by his contention that "power is everywhere."

9. See, e.g., Freeman v. Berge, 441 F.3d 543 (7th Cir. 2006) (discussing prison's feeding rule requiring that, when meals were delivered to an inmate's cell, the inmate had to be wearing trousers or gym shorts in light of security issues and respect for female security officers' privacy, and determining that prison officials' withholding of food from an inmate when he wore a sock on his head when meals were delivered to his cell did not constitute the use of food deprivation as punishment, for purposes of Eighth Amendment prohibition against cruel and unusual punishment, and was a reasonable condition to the receipt of food, in light of security issues presented by the possibility that the sock could be used as a weapon if something was inside it).

10. Note that the timing of meals may differ from institution to institution, but that virtually all prisons serve evening meals at early times. Some jurisdictions in the United States recognize the difficulty of lengthy waits between the evening and morning meal and legislate maximum gaps. Under Nebraska law, for example, the breakfast meal shall be served not more than fifteen hours following

the previous day's evening meal (81 NE ADC Ch. 11, § 002). In California, no more than fourteen hours may elapse between the evening meal and breakfast in jail (15 CA ADC § 3050(a)(2)).

11. In late 2005, Padilla was indicted on terrorism conspiracy charges that do not include the dirty bomb plot.

12. US Const. Amend. I.

13. Turner v. Safley, 482 U.S. 78, 84 (1987); see also Sunshine (1983, 439), who states that "the prisoner . . . does not shed all of his rights at the prison gate."

14. Safley, 482 at 95.

15. *Id.* at 84-85.

16. *Id.* at 89.

17. *Id.* at 89-90.

18. *Id.* at 90.

19. *Id.*

20. *Id.*

21. 227 F.3d 47, 59 (3d Cir. 2000).

22. *Id.* at 52-53.

23. *Id.* at 54.

24. *Id.* at 56 n.4.

25. *Id.* at 59-60.

26. 343 F.3d 212, 215-16 (3d Cir. 2003).

27. *Id.* at 217-19.

28. *Id.* at 219.

29. *Id.* at 219-21.

30. *Id.* at 221.

31. *Id.* at 221-22.

32. In contrast, relatives of prisoners in Goma, Congo, are permitted to bring food to their loved ones. But war in the region makes visits difficult and without food from relatives or handouts from good Samaritans, prisoners must rely on food from the government, which is delivered erratically to prison authorities (who themselves face hunger because of lengthy delays in paychecks). As Lacey (2004) describes, "If there is a worse place on earth than a Congolese prison, stay well away. The prisons in this country are dank, violent places. A prisoner can spend years in a cell with only the vaguest notion of what he did to get thrown inside. The punishment for many, regardless of the crime, can be slowly wasting, by starving to death."

33. The expensive food from prison snack machines, combined with the costs incurred for traveling to prisons (many are located in rural areas far from urban areas, necessitating lengthy trips and overnight stays) creates obstacles for families and friends wishing to visit inmates. Tewksbury and DeMichele (2005, 295, 308) suggest that such impediments may be counterproductive given that "an inmate's connection with the outside, through visitation programs, could greatly reduce inmate tensions and in turn reduce the likelihood of riots, disturbances, and deviant behavior," and that "inmates receiving visitors are found to better integrate themselves into society on release, hence reducing their potential to recidivate." See also *id.* at 294, 308 (noting the "powerful potential possessed by family visitation programs to maintain inmates' social ties with their families through visits" and the fact that visitation programs "are related to enhanced social adjustment for both the period of incarceration and release," and pointing to studies that have found a "reduction of institutional infractions and diminished perceptions of overcrowding on the part

of those receiving visitors during their incarceration"); see generally Domanick (2004, 231-39); Grinstead et al. (2001, 59-60).

34. For a brief explanation of when the last meal tradition began, see, e.g., Treadwell (2001, 64); Black (2003, 9). For a somewhat humorous fictional account by a death row chef, see Giles Smith (2000).

35 Cf. Black (2003, 20), who claims that "no dollar limit is placed on an inmate's last meal request. But food items must be readily available in the prison kitchen." Price (2005) notes, however, that staff members would sometimes purchase items that were unavailable at the prison kitchen commissary and give them to Price to prepare for the inmate's last meal.

36. Two sources suggest that Castillo actually received twenty-four tacos, in addition to two cheeseburgers, two whole onions, five jalapeno peppers, six enchiladas, six tostadas, one quart of milk, and one chocolate milkshake (Treadwell and Vernon 2001, 37-38; Black 2003, 60-61.

37. According to Treadwell and Vernon (2001, 142), Virginia is the only state where the condemned inmate may keep his or her choice of a last meal hidden from the press.

38. In another example of spectacle, then-Governor Bill Clinton interrupted his New Hampshire primary campaign in 1992 to fly home to Arkansas to preside over the execution of Rickey Ray Rector—a man so severely brain-damaged (his attorney referred to him as "truly zombied out" and "a human blank") that he saved his pecan pie for after his execution and indicated that he would vote for Clinton even after his request for clemency was rejected (and despite the fact that Arkansas prisoners, like those in forty-seven other states, are barred from voting while incarcerated). That Arkansas law did not require Clinton's presence in the state for the execution adds to

the argument that such an act served as a political display of toughness on crime (Cohen 1993; Frady 1993; Coyne and Entzeroth 1996, 43-44; Entzeroth 2002, 307n64; Sifakis 2003, 216-17).

39. For some inmates, the infantilization continues even after they are released. Because ex-offenders frequently encounter difficulties finding housing and employment upon reentry (see, e.g., Brisman 2004, 2007), many former inmates wind up in homeless shelters where they are subject to "parental" treatment by staff (Dejarlais 1996, 884).

40. Note that in sub-Saharan African countries such as Sierra Leone and Uganda, government food deliveries to prisons are erratic. When there is no food, prisoners frequently attempt to escape. When there is food, prisoners are less inclined to attempt escape (Wines 2006). Such a phenomenon is familiar in discourses about power. As Ortner (1995, 175) explains, "the dominant often has something to offer, and sometimes a great deal (though always of course at the price of continuing in power). The subordinate thus has many grounds for ambivalence about resisting the relationship."

41. The hierarchic character of Tudor England was reflected in its cuisine. In fact, in May 1517, Henry VIII issued a royal proclamation that dictated in minute detail the number and composition of dishes suitable for important persons, with cardinals at the top (Hammer 1999, 664).

42. Writing more broadly, Ortner (1995, 175) contends that "there is never a single, unitary, subordinate, if only in the simple sense that subaltern groups are internally divided by age, gender, status, and other forms of difference and that occupants of differing subject positions will have different, even opposed, but still legitimate perspectives on the situation." This is not to suggest, of course, that collective resistance is impossible. Despite Sykes' (1958) generally

correct observation that the ethos of distrust and individualism in prison mitigates against the kind of inmate cooperation necessary to rebel, Valentine and Longstaff (1998, 145) note, "Food is such an important part of the material culture of the prison . . . that grievances about food can spark rioting and collective action by the inmates to overpower the officers." And Garland (1990, 172) explains, "In many disciplinary situations, such as the monastery, the school, or the factory, the individual co-operates in his training because, at least to some extent, he shares the goals of the disciplinary process (to overcome the flesh, to become educated, to earn a wage). The key problem for the prison as a form of discipline is that individual prisoners may have no inclination and no need to take an active part in the process. . . . Resistance to official authority occurs most frequently and most effectively in those prisons where an alternative inmate culture offers oppositional identifications, roles, and forms of support for those who adopt them."

43. Note, however, that food fantasies, if shared with other inmates, can offer prisoners a psychological escape and foster a sense of camaraderie. In Frank McGuinness' play, *Someone Who'll Watch Over Me*, the characters Adam, Edward, and Michael have all been kidnapped and imprisoned in Lebanon. To help overcome the loneliness and despair of their condition, the three pretend to drink alcoholic beverages, with Edward playing the role of bartender, serving martinis and sherries (McGuinness 1992, Act. I, Scene 5).

44. 378 U.S. 546 (1964).

45. Jones v. Bock, 549 US (2007). The Supreme Court noted that this number excludes habeas corpus petitions and motions to vacate a sentence. If these filings are included, prisoner complaints constituted 24 percent of all civil filings in 2005. *Id.* at n.1. For a brief discussion of this case, see Greenhouse (2007).

46. It bears mention that some cases may be considered frivolous or otherwise lacking in merit simply because prisoners frequently lack the funds to hire counsel and must file their complaints pro se.

47. 110 Stat. 1321–71, as amended, 42 U. S. C. §1997e et seq.

48. Like a "hunger strike," a "death fast" may also involve the ingestion of water, salt, sugar, and vitamin B1 in order to decrease the chance of permanent nutritional disability (such as neuropathy or congestive heart failure) (Oguz and Miles 2005, 169). But in contrast to the hunger striker, the death faster "asserts that the fasting will continue to death unless the aims of the strike are met." As the authors further explain, "Most hunger strikers are trying to effect political change rather than trying to become martyrs, commit suicide, or maim themselves with nutritional deficiencies. A death fast increases the pressure on the negotiation."

49. The issue of whether a prisoner has a right to bring about his own death has recently arisen in a different context—capital cases. Some inmates, unwilling to spend years on death row while their attorneys pursue appeals on "little procedural errors," have argued for the right to withdraw appeals (Liptak 2007, A14)—a position that is gaining support among some scholars (see, e.g., Blume 2005; Blank 2006).

50. Cave (2006, WK4) presents slightly different data, claiming that Gandhi survived seventeen hunger strikes during his campaign for India's independence from Britain.

51. Scott Anderson (2001, 42-47, 74, 124-25) notes that the 2001 strikers learned a lot from the 1996 hunger strikers, including ways to slow down muscular atrophy. Although techniques such as replacing sodium chloride with potassium chloride and refined sugar with crude sugar help reduce daily weight loss, which is important if the

strike ends, prolonged "ketosis" or "self-cannibalization"—the process by which the human body metabolizes its own proteins for food during the prolonged absence of normal nutrition (Sunshine 1983, 426 n.40) —is exponentially more painful.

52. Scott Anderson (2001, 42-47, 74, 124-25) explains that under Turkish government policy, hunger-striking prisoners are often granted medical leave in the hope that the freedom will make them quit their strikes; they are then reincarcerated when they recover. Great Britain has also tried this approach (Ludwig 1983, 171).

53. Scott Anderson (2001, 42-47, 74, 124-25) adds that the "advancements" in fasting techniques (see n.50) lead to intense hunger, the excruciating ache of muscle deterioration and constriction, followed by the internal bleeding of organs—making it too hard for an individual to bear by himself or herself and virtually necessitating a collective approach.

54. For a history of force-feeding in the United States, see Bennett (1983, 1159n4).

55. Note, however, that A. Eves and B. Gesch (2003), in a study of 159 British prisoners between the ages of eighteen and twenty-one, found that the food provided to the prisoners by the prison kitchen met nutritional requirements but that the quality of the actual diet consumed, which was determined by the choices made by the prisoners (i.e., extra items purchased from the prison shop), often revealed poor food choices (e.g., fat intake exceeding the recommended percentage, low intake of Vitamin D, sodium in excess of the recommended amount.

56. Similarly, Sifakis (2003, 281) discusses the need of prisoners to exercise because prisons offer a sedentary environment with food that is often high in fat and cholesterol.

57. The federal Bureau of Prisons and twenty-three state corrections departments have policies that expressly allow restraints during labor. California and Illinois are the only two states with laws forbidding the practice of shackling prisoners during labor (Liptak 2006).

58. Cf. C. Smith (2002, 199), who contends that prison health promotion initiatives "may go some way towards preventing the revolving door syndrome, encouraging women to adopt a 'healthier lifestyle' following discharge from prison."

Works Cited

Abramsky, Sasha. 2006. *Conned: How Millions West to Prison, Lost the Vote, and Helped Send George W. Bush to the White House*. New York: New Press.

Abu-Lughod, Lila. 1990. "The Romance of Resistance: Tracing Transformations of Power through Bedouin Women." *American Ethnologist* 17(1): 41-55.

Agnew, Robert. 1992. "Foundation for a General Theory of Strain." *Criminology* 30(1): 47-87.

———. 2006. *Pressured Into Crime: An Overview of General Strain Theory*. Los Angeles: Roxbury.

Allen, Nancy. 1994. "Composting Food Scraps at Georgia Prison." *BioCycle* 35(4): 90.

Anderson, Lloyd C. 2000. *Voices from a Southern Prison*. Athens, GA: University of Georgia Press.

Anderson, Scott. 2001. "The Hunger Warriors." *New York Times Magazine*, October 21, 42-47, 74, 124-25.

Angelo and Temporary Services. 2003. *Prisoners' Inventions*. Chicago: WhiteWalls.

Ansbacher, Richard. 1983. "Force-Feeding Hunger-Striking Prisoners: A Framework for Analysis." *University of Florida Law Review* 35(1): 99-129.

Arens, W., and Ivan Karp. 1989. *Creativity of Power: Cosmology and Action in African Societies*. Washington: Smithsonian Institution Press.

Becker, Elizabeth, and Ginger Thompson. 2003. "Poorer Nations Plead Farmers' Case at Trade Talks." *New York Times*, September 11, A3.

Bennett, Stephen C. 1983. "The Privacy and Procedural Due Process Rights of Hunger Striking Prisoners. *New York University Law Review* 58:1157-1230.

Benyon, Joe. 1996. "Hunger Strike in Turkish Prisons." *Lancet* 348(9029): 737.

Black, Jacquelyn C. 2003. . . . *Last Meal*. Monroe, ME: Common Courage Press.

Blank, Stephen. 2006. "Killing Time: The Process of Waiving Appeal: The Michael Ross Death Penalty Cases." *Journal of Law and Policy* 14:735-777.

Block, Dave. 1997. "Composting Prison Food Residuals." *BioCycle* 38(8): 37-39.

Blume, John H. 2005. "Killing the Willing: 'Volunteers,' Suicide and Competency." *Michigan Law Review* 103:939-1009.

Blumenthal, Ralph. 2007. "U.S. Gives Tour of Family Detention Center That Critics Liken to a Prison." *New York Times*, February 10, A9.

Bourdieu, Pierre. 2000. "The Aesthetic Sense as the Sense of Distinction." In *The Consumer Society Reader*, edited by Juliet B. Schor and Douglas B. Holt, 205-211. New York: New Press.

Brisman, Avi. 2004. "Double Whammy: Collateral Consequences of Conviction and Imprisonment for Sustainable Communities and the Environment." *William and Mary Environmental Law and Policy Review* 28(2): 423-75.

———. 2007. "Toward a More Elaborate Typology of Environmental Values: Liberalizing Criminal Disenfranchisement Laws and Policies." *New England Journal on Criminal & Civil Confinement* 33(2): 283-454.

Brown, Patricia Leigh. 2006. "A Rare Kind of Food Bank, and Just Maybe the Hippest, Flourishes." *New York Times*, September 26, A17.

Burton-Rose, Daniel. 1998. "Solidarity in Stillwater: The Oak Park Heights Prisoner Work Strike." In *The Celling of America: An Inside Look at the U.S. Prison Industry*, edited by Daniel Burton-Rose, Dan Pens, and Paul Wright, 127-31. Monroe, ME: Common Courage Press.

———. 2003. "Work Strike Suppressed and Sabotaged in Ohio." In *Prison Nation: The Warehousing of America's Poor*, edited by Tara Herivel and Paul Wright, 129-132. New York: Routledge.

———, Dan Pens, and Paul Wright, eds. 1998. *The Celling of America: An Inside Look at the U.S. Prison Industry*. Monroe, ME: Common Courage Press.

Cahill, Danny. 1998. "The Global Economy Behind Ohio Prison Walls." In *The Celling of America: An Inside Look at the U.S. Prison Industry*, edited by Daniel Burton-Rose, Dan Pens and Paul Wright, 109-111. Monroe, ME: Common Courage Press.

———, and Paul Wright. 1998. "Worked to Death." In *The Celling of America: An Inside Look at the U.S. Prison Industry*, edited by Daniel Burton-Rose, Dan Pens, and Paul Wright, 112-113. Monroe, ME: Common Courage Press.

Cantor, Norman L. 1973. "A Patient's Decision to Decline Life-Saving Medical Treatment: Bodily Integrity Versus the Preservation of Life." *Rutgers Law Review* 26:228-264.

Carr, Coeli. 2006. "A Paper Jailbird in Every Cell." *New York Times*, March 19, AR4.

Cave, Damien. 2006. "As a Tactic, Starving is Found Wanting." *New York Times*, July 30, WK4.

Chaudhry, Rajan. 1991. "Splatter-Proof Meals Await Sentencing. (Prison Food Baked into Loaves)." September. http://findarticles.com/p/articles/mi_hb3402/ is_199109/ ai_n8157629.

Chivers, C.J. 2006. "Hundreds Disappear Into the Black Hole of the Kurdish Prison System in Iraq." *New York Times*, December 26, A18.

Cohen, Richard. 1993. "The Execution of Rickey Ray Rector." *Washington Post*, February 23, A19.

Coyne, Randall, and Lyn Entzeroth. 1996. "Report Regarding Implementation of the American Bar Association's Recommendations and Resolutions Concerning the Death Penalty and Calling for a Moratorium on Executions." *Georgetown Journal on Fighting Poverty* 4:3-51.

Crawford, Amanda J., and Chip Scutari. 2003. "Private-Prisons Proposal on Table." *Arizona Republic*, November 19.

Cusac, Anne-Marie. 2003. "'The Judge Gave Me Ten Years. He Didn't Sentence Me to Death': Prisoners with HIV Deprived of Proper Care." In *Prison Nation: The Warehousing of America's Poor*, edited by Tara Herivel and Paul Wright, 195-203. New York: Routledge.

Daly, Martin, and Margo Wilson. 1997. "Crime and Conflict: Homicide in Evolutionary Psychological Perspective." *Crime & Justice* 22:51-100.

Dejarlais, Robert. 1996. "The Office of Reason: On the Politics of Language and Agency in a Shelter for 'The Homeless Mentally Ill.'" *American Ethnologist* 23(4): 880-900.

Dewan, Shaila. 2006. "100 Pounds Lighter; With Advice to Share." *New York Times*, September 10, 16.

Domanick, Joe. 2004. *Cruel Justice: Three Strikes and the Politics of Crime in America's Golden State*. Berkeley: University of California Press.

Dostoyevsky, Fyodor. 1957. *The House of the Dead*. Translated by Constance Garnett. New York: Heinemann.

Dow, Mark. 2003. "'Make It Hard for Them': A Hunger Strike Against the INS." In *Prison Nation: The Warehousing of America's Poor*, edited by Tara Herivel and Paul Wright, 269-273. New York: Routledge.

Dreeben, Michael R. 2006. "The Right to Present a Twinkie Defense." *Green Bag* 2d. ser. 9(4): 347-52.

Durland, Steven. 1998. "Maintaining Humanity: An Interview with Grady Hillman about Arts-in-Corrections." In *The Citizen Artist: 20 Years of Art in the Public Arena: An Anthology from High Performance Magazine 1978-1998*. Vol. 1, edited by Linda Frye Burnham and Steven Durland, 251-58. Gardiner, NY: Critical Press.

Editorial. 2005. "Death Behind Bars." *New York Times*, March 10, A24.

Editorial. 2006. "Giving Birth in Chains." *New York Times*, March 15, WK13.

Editorial. 2007. "The Future of Farming." *New York Times*, February 17, A26.

Entzeroth, Lyn. 2002. "Constitutional Prohibition on the Execution of the Mentally Retarded Criminal Defendant." *Tulsa Law Review* 38:299-327.

Erikson, Erik H. 1969. *Gandhi's Truth: On the Origins of Militant Nonviolence*. New York: W. W. Norton.

Eves, A., and B. Gesch. 2003. "Food Provision and the Nutritional Implications of Food Choices Made by Young Adult Males, in a Young Offenders' Institution." *Journal of Human Nutrition and Dietetics* 16(3): 167-79.

Ferrell, Jeff. 1994. "Confronting the Agenda of Authority: Critical Criminology, Anarchism, and Urban Graffiti." In *Varieties of Criminology: Readings from a Dynamic Discipline*, edited by Gregg Barak, 161-78. Westport, CT: Praeger.

Fleetwood, Blake. 1987. "From the People Who Brought You the Twinkie Defense; The Rise of the Expert Witness Industry." *Washington Monthly*, June, 33.

"Force Feeding." *New Law Journal* 124(February 7): 113.

Foucault, Michel. 1977. *Discipline and Punish: The Birth of a Prison*. Translated by Alan Sheridan. New York: Vintage Books.

———. 1978. *The History of Sexuality. Vol. I: An Introduction*. Translated by Robert Hurley. New York: Vintage Books.

Frady, Marshall. 1993. "Death In Arkansas." *New Yorker*, February 22, 105-33.

Garland, David. 1990. *Punishment and Modern Society: A Study in Social Theory.* Chicago: University of Chicago Press.

Gesch, B., S. Hammon, S. Hampson, A. Eves, and M. Crowder. 2002. "Influence of Supplementary Vitamins, Minerals and Fatty Acids on the Antisocial Behaviour of Young Adult Prisoners." *British Journal of Psychiatry* 18:22-28.

Godderis, Rebecca. 2006. "Dining In: The Symbolic Power of Food in Prison." *Howard Journal of Criminal Justice* 43(3): 255-67.

Golden, Tim. 2006. "Military Taking a Tougher Line With Detainees." *New York Times*, December 16, A1, A12.

Greenberg, Joel K. 1983. "Hunger Striking Prisoners: The Constitutionality of Force-Feeding." *Fordham Law Review* 51: 747-70.

Greenhouse, Linda. 2007. "Limits on Prison Suits Are Eased." *New York Times*, January 23, A15.

Grinstead, O., B. Faigeles, C. Bancroft, and B. Zack. 2001. "The Financial Cost of Maintaining Relationships with Incarcerated African American Men: A Survey of Women Prison Visitors. *Journal of African-American Men* 6(1): 59-69.

Hammer, Carl I. 1999. "A Hearty Meal? The Prison Diets of Cranmer and Latimer." *Sixteenth Century Journal* 30(3): 653-680.

Haskell, Kari. 2003. "Hope After a Life Haunted By Drugs and Mental Illness." *New York Times*, Wednesday, December 17, C23.

Herivel, Tara. 2003. "Wreaking Medical Mayhem on Women Prisoners in Washington State. In *Prison Nation: The Warehousing of America's Poor,*" edited by Tara Herivel and Paul Wright, 174-80. New York: Routledge.

Hibbeln, Joseph R., J. C. Umhau, M. Linniola, D. T. George, P. W. Ragan, S. E. Shoaf, M. R. Vaughan, R. Rawlings, and N. Salem, Jr. 1998. "A Replication Study of Violent and Nonviolent Subjects: Cerebrospinal Fluid Metabolites of Serotonin and Dopamine Are Predicted by Plasma Essential Fatty Acids." *Biological Society* 44:243-49.

Hillman, Grady. 2002. "The Mythology of the Corrections Community." In *Teaching the Arts in Prison*, edited by Rachel Marie-Cane Williams, 14-27. Boston: Northeastern University Press.

Inciardi, James A., Duane C. McBride, and James E. Rivers. 1996. *Drug Control and the Courts*. Vol. 3 of *Drugs, Health, and Social Policy Series*. Thousand Oaks, CA: Sage Publications.

Lacey, Marc. 2004. "Making Hard Time Even Harder: Let the Inmates Starve." *New York Times*, December 31, A4.

Lafer, Gordon. 2003. "The Politics of Prison Labor: A Union Perspective." In *Prison Nation: The Warehousing of America's Poor*, edited by Tara Herivel and Paul Wright, 120-28. New York: Routledge.

Levassuer, Raymond Luc. 1998. "Armed and Dangerous." In *The Celling of America: An Inside Look at the U.S. Prison Industry*, edited by Daniel Burton-Rose, Dan Pens, and Paul Wright, 122-26. Monroe, ME: Common Courage Press.

Levister, Chris. 2006. "Inside Jobs—Convict Rehab or Corporate Slavery?" *Black Voice News*, August 7. http://news.newamericamedia.org/ news/view_article.html?article_id =22f7bb08424eb621764333f9e6c211d8 and http://www.truthout.org/issues_06/091406LB.shtml.

Liptak, Adam. 2006a. "Pregnant Inmates Often Shackled During Labor." *New York Times*, March 2, A1, A21.

———. 2006b. "In Prison for Life, He Turns M&M's Into an Art Form." *New York Times*, July 21, A1, A17.

———. 2006c. "Prison Disciplines Publicized Inmate Who Makes Art Using M&M's." *New York Times*, August 4, A12.

———. 2007. "Another Kind of Appeal From Death Row: Kill Me." *New York Times*, March 12, A14.

Livingston, Jay. 1996. *Crime and Criminology*. 2nd ed. Upper Saddle River, NJ: Prentice Hall.

Lomax, Adrian. 1998. "Varied Forms of Rebellion and Resistance: Nonviolent Protest Suppressed." In *The Celling of America: An Inside Look at the U.S. Prison Industry*, edited by Daniel Burton-Rose, Dan Pens, and Paul Wright, 225-27. Monroe, ME: Common Courage Press.

―――. 2003. "Prison Jobs and Free Market Employment." In *Prison Nation: The Warehousing of America's Poor*, edited by Tara Herivel and Paul Wright, 133-35. New York: Routledge.

Ludwig, Glenn Allan. 1983. "Hunger Striking: Freedom of Choice or the State's Best Interest." *New England Journal on Criminal and Civil Confinement* 10:169-92.

Lupton, D. 1996. *Food, the Body and the Self*. London: Sage.

Mandela, Nelson. 2000. *Long Walk to Freedom*. New York: Holt, Rinehart and Winston.

Martin, Roderick. 1971. "The Concept of Power: A Critical Defence." *British Journal of Sociology* 22(3): 240-256.

Martin, Sandra L., H. Kim, L. L. Kupper, R. E. Meyer, and M. Hays. 1997. "Is Incarceration during Pregnancy Associated with Infant Birthweight?" *American Journal of Public Health* 87(9): 1526-531.

Masha, Lebofsa. 2004. Constitution Hill Tour Captures Essence of SA." http://www.jda.org.za/constitutionhill/5may04_conhill_essence. stm.

McGuinness, Frank. 2002. *Plays Two: Mary and Lizie, Someone Who'll Watch Over Me, Dolly West's Kitchen, The Bird Sanctuary*. London: Faber and Faber.

Mihm, Stephen. 2006. "Does Eating Salmon Lower the Murder Rate?" *New York Times Magazine*, April 16, 18.

Mintz, Sidney Wilfred. 1985. *Sweetness and Power: The Place of Sugar in Modern History*. New York: Viking.

Morse, Margaret. 1994. "'What Do Cyborgs Eat?': Oral Logic in an Information Society." *Discourse* 16(3): 86-123.

Nagin, Daniel S. 1998. "Criminal Deterrence Research at the Outset of the Twenty-first Century." *Crime and Justice: A Review of Research* 23:1-42.

Oguz, N.Y. and S. H. Miles. 2005. "The Physician and Prison Hunger Strikes: Reflecting on the Experience in Turkey." *Journal of Medical Ethics* 31:169-72.

Ortner, Sherry B. 1995. "Resistance and the Problem of Ethnographic Refusal." *Comparative Studies in Society and History.* 37(1): 173-93.

Oshinsky, David M. 1997. *"Worse Than Slavery": Parchman Farm and the Ordeal of Jim Crow Justice.* New York: Simon and Schuster.

Pens, Dan. 1998a. "Kidnapping and Extortion, Texas-Style." In *The Celling of America: An Inside Look at the U.S. Prison Industry*, edited by Daniel Burton-Rose, Dan Pens, and Paul Wright, 149-52. Monroe, ME: Common Courage Press.

———. 1998b. "Microsoft 'Outcells' Competition." In *The Celling of America: An Inside Look at the U.S. Prison Industry*, edited by Daniel Burton-Rose, Dan Pens, and Paul Wright, 114-21. Monroe, ME: Common Courage Press.

———. 1998c. "Texas Prisoners Build Their Own Cages." In *The Celling of America: An Inside Look at the U.S. Prison Industry*, edited by Daniel Burton-Rose, Dan Pens, and Paul Wright, 107-08. Monroe, ME: Common Courage Press.

———. 1998d. "VitaPro Fraud in Texas." In *The Celling of America: An Inside Look at the U.S. Prison Industry*, edited by Daniel Burton-Rose, Dan Pens, and Paul Wright, 147-48. Monroe, ME: Common Courage Press.

Pfeiffer, Mary Beth. 2004. "A Death in the Box." *New York Times Magazine*, October 31, 48-53.

Pogash, Carol. 2003. "The Myth of the 'Twinkie Defense': The Verdict in the Dan White Case Wasn't Based on his Consumption of Junk Food." *San Francisco Chronicle*, November 23, D1.

Powell, Stephanie Clavan. 1983. "Forced Feeding of a Prisoner on a Hunger Strike: A Violation of an Inmate's Right to Privacy." *North Carolina Law Review* 61:714-32.

Price, Brian D. 2004. "The Last Supper." *Legal Affairs* March/April, 31.

———. 2005. *Meals to Die For*. London: Artnik.

Rabinow, Paul, ed. 1984. *The Foucault Reader*. New York: Pantheon Books.

Rhodes, Lorna A. 2004. *Total Confinement: Madness and Reason in the Maximum Security Prison*. Berkeley: University of California Press.

Rosenberg, Tina. 2003. "Why Mexico's Small Corn Farmers Go Hungry." *New York Times*, March 3, A22.

Said, Edward W. 1986. "Foucault and the Imagination of Power." In *Foucault: A Critical Reader*, edited by David Couzens Hoy, 149-55. Oxford: Basil Blackwell.

Schrift, Melissa. 2006. "Angola Prison Art: Captivity, Creativity, and Consumerism." *Journal of American Folklore* 119(473): 257-74.

Shafer, N.E. 1991. "Prison Visiting Policies and Practices." *International Journal of Offender Therapy and Comparative Criminology* 35:263-275.

"Sheriff Runs Female Chain Gang." 2003. Reuters. Oct. 29. CNN.com. http://www.cnn.com/2003/US/Southwest/10/29/chain.gang.reut/.

Sherwood, Mark, and Bob Posey. 2003. "FDOC Hazardous to Prisoners' Health." In *Prison Nation: The Warehousing of America's Poor*, edited by Tara Herivel and Paul Wright, 204-9. New York: Routledge.

Sifakis, Carl. 2003. *The Encyclopedia of American Prisons*. New York: Facts on File, Inc.

Silver, Mara. 2005. "Testing Cruzan: Prisoners and the Constitutional Question of Self-Starvation." *Stanford Law Review* 58:631-62.

Silverstein, Ken. 1998. "America's Private Gulag." In *The Celling of America: An Inside Look at the U.S. Prison Industry*, edited by Daniel Burton-Rose, Dan Pens, and Paul Wright, 156-63. Monroe, ME: Common Courage Press.

Smith, Catrin. 2002. "Punishment and Pleasure: Women, Food and the Imprisoned Body." *Sociological Review* 50(2): 197-214.

Smith, Giles. 2000. "Last Requests." In *Speaking with the Angel: Original Stories*, edited by Nicholas Hornby, 31-43. New York: Riverhead Books.

Smith, Roger. 2005. "Washington Prison's Water System and Meat Contaminated With Feces." *Prison Legal News* 16(1): 19.

Sneed, D., and Harry W. Stonecipher. 1989. "Prisoner Fasting as Symbolic Speech: The Ultimate Speech-Action Test." *Howard Law Journal* 32:549-62.

Sontag, Deborah. 2006. "Videotape Offers a Window Into a Terror Suspect's Isolation." *New York Times*, December 4, A1, A22.

St. Clair, Jeffrey. 2003. "Bill Clinton's Blood Trails." *Prison Nation: The Warehousing of America's Poor*, edited by Tara Herivel and Paul Wright, 210-13. New York: Routledge.

Stough, O'Neil, and Dan Pens. 1998. "Oppression on the Rise in Arizona." In *The Celling of America: An Inside Look at the U.S. Prison Industry*, edited by Daniel Burton-Rose, Dan Pens, and Paul Wright, 64-69. Monroe, ME: Common Courage Press.

Sunshine, Steven C. 1983. "Should a Hunger-Striking Prisoner Be Allowed to Die?" *Boston College Law Review* 51:423-58.

Sykes, Gresham. 1958. "The Pains of Imprisonment." In *The Society of Captives: A Study of Maximum Security Prison*, edited by Gresham M. Sykes, 62-83. Princeton: Princeton University Press.

Talvi, Silja J.A. 2003. "Hepatitis C: A 'Silent Epidemic' Strikes U.S. Prisons." In *Prison Nation: The Warehousing of America's Poor*, edited by Tara Herivel and Paul Wright, 181-86. New York: Routledge.

Tewksbury, Richard, and Matthew DeMichele. 2005. "Going to Prison: A Prison Visitation Program." *The Prison Journal* 85(3): 292-310.

Thompson, James. 2002. "Doubtful Principles in Arts in Prisons." In *Teaching the Arts in Prison*, edited by Rachel Marie-Cane Williams, 40-61. Boston: Northeastern University Press.

Treadwell, Ty, and Michelle Vernon. 2001. *Last Suppers: Famous Final Meals from Death Row*. Port Townsend, WA: Loompanics Unlimited.

Urbina, Ian. 2006. "Panel Suggests Using Inmates In Drug Trials." *New York Times*. August 13, A1.

Valentine, Gill, and Beth Longstaff. 1998. "Doing Porridge: Food and Social Relations in a Male Prison." *Journal of Material Culture* 3(2): 131-52.

Visser, Margaret. 1991. *The Rituals of Dinner*. Toronto: HarperCollins.

von Zielbauer, Paul. 2005a. "As Health Care in Jails Goes Private, 10 Days Can Be a Death Sentence." *New York Times*, February 27, A1, A26-28.

———. 2005b. "Missed Signals in New York Jails Open Way to Season of Suicides." *New York Times*, February 28, A1, A18-19.

———. 2005c. "A Spotty Record of Health Care At Juvenile Sites in New York." *New York Times*, March 1, A1, A20.

Wakeen, Barbara. 2006. "Food Service and Nutrition Standards—What Jail Administrators Need to Know." *American Jails* 19(6): 49-51.

Washington, Harriet A. 2007. *Medical Apartheid: The Dark History of Medical Experimentation on Black Americans from Colonial Times to the Present*. New York: Doubleday.

"Waste Wood, Food Rejects Make Great Combo at County/State Prison Site." 2001. *BioCycle* 42(7): 19.

Weber, Max. 1947. *The Theory of Social and Economic Organization*. Translated by A. M. Henderson and T. Parson. Glencoe: Free Press.

Williams, Rachel Marie-Cane. 2002a. "Entering the Circle: The Praxis of Arts in Corrections." *Journal of Arts Management, Law, and Society* 31(4): 293-303.

———. 2002b. Introduction to *Teaching the Arts in Prison*, edited by Rachel Marie-Cane Williams, 3-13. Boston: Northeastern University Press.

———. 2002c. "Learning to Teach by Traveling Inside: The Experience and Process of Mural Making in a Women's Correctional Facility." In *Teaching the Arts in Prison*, edited by Rachel Marie-Cane Williams, 138-52. Boston: Northeastern University Press.

———, and Janette Y. Taylor. 2004. "Narrative Art and Incarcerated Abused Women." *Art Education* 57(2): 46-52.

Wines, Michael. 2006. "For Young Offenders, Justice as Impoverished as Africa." *New York Times*, December 24, 1, 13.

Wisely, Willie. 2003. "Corcoran: Sex, Lies, and Videotapes." In *Prison Nation: The Warehousing of America's Poor*, edited by Tara Herivel and Paul Wright, 245-52. New York: Routledge.

———. 2003b. "The New Bedlam." In *Prison Nation: The Warehousing of America's Poor*, edited by Tara Herivel and Paul Wright, 168-73. New York: Routledge.

Wolf, Eric. R. 1990. "Distinguished Lecture: Facing Power." *American Anthropologist* 92(3): 586-96.

Woods, Chuck. 2004. "Seminole County Inmates Raise 'Beneficial Bugs' for UF and USDA Researchers." *University of Florida News*. http://news.ufl. edu/2004/11/08/prison-bigs/

———. 2005. Bailed Out by BUGS. *American Vegetable Grower*. http://www.allbusiness.com/agriculture-forestry/crop-production-vegetable/978091-1.html.

Wright, Paul. 1998a. "Clallam Prisoners—'No Grievances'?" In *The Celling of America: An Inside Look at the U.S. Prison Industry*, edited by Daniel Burton-Rose, Dan Pens, and Paul Wright, 36-39. Monroe, ME: Common Courage Press.

———.1998b. "Slaves of the State." In *The Celling of America: An Inside Look at the U.S. Prison Industry*, edited by Daniel Burton-Rose, Dan Pens, and Paul Wright, 102-06. Monroe, ME: Common Courage Press.

———. 2003. "Making Slave Labor Fly: Boeing Goes to Prison." In *Prison Nation: The Warehousing of America's Poor*, edited by Tara Herivel and Paul Wright, 112-19. New York: Routledge.

Young, Ronald. 2003. "Dying for Profits." In *Prison Nation: The Warehousing of America's Poor*, edited by Tara Herivel and Paul Wright, 187-94. New York: Routledge.

Teaching Anthropology Through Food
David M. Johnson

Introduction

My goal here is to share some ideas that I have learned about the teaching and learning process and to apply them to a specific course where I used food as a teaching tool. Before I do the review, let me say a few words about why it is fun and useful to teach with food. Others can come up with their own ideas, but here are some of mine:

> 1. Use the fact that everybody eats! Since everyone eats, all students will have experience with food and food preparation from at least one tradition, so they will be able to relate their experience to the course materials. *Everybody Eats!* is actually the title of a book I used for the course. (See Anderson 2005.)
>
> 2. When teaching with food, it is easy to make comparisons between: (a) cultural groups, (b) food types, and (c) cultural preferences.
>
> 3. There are also lots of foodways available, and they are often highly visible and easy to find.

The subject should be accessible to students and faculty and provide many ways to make comparisons and generate hypotheses about human behavior.

Pedgagogy

Until recently the term *pedagogy* was not one I used often. Usually it had some vaguely obscene connotations, like "matriculation," and hence was not something that one would say in the presence of one's mother (and perhaps not in front of one's colleagues).

In terms of pedagogy, I count myself as a long-time practitioner of what I call the "Table of Contents" School of Course Design. This system makes it easy to design a course; all the instructor does is open the textbook to the Table of Contents, count the number of chapters, and then, depending on the number of them, make each chapter the topic for a week's worth of classes.

For example, if the text is divided into sixteen chapters, and there are sixteen weeks in the semester, then one chapter is assigned for each week. Simple. All the instructor needs to do is put in some material about office hours, grading system, and related information, and Presto! The syllabus is complete.

The catch here is that the syllabus, and hence the course, is designed solely around content. Issues about student learning and how best to formulate what the instructor wants to accomplish for the semester, are not dealt with at all.

Although I had been a long-time practitioner of this method, I was not always comfortable with it. While I made modifications to my syllabi and teaching methods that I thought were improvements, I was not aware of the scholarship of teaching and learning.

In the past few years, my campus, North Carolina A&T State University, has been blessed with a formal Academy for Teaching and Learning, currently led by the dynamic Dr. Scott Simkins, a reformed economist. He sponsors workshops and lectures by noted scholars in the area of teaching and learning, building on a tradition established by the Director of the University's Honors Program, Dr. Meyers. Through my attendance at these activities, I have come to learn more about alternatives to Table of Contents Pedagogy. I will discuss some of the workshop leaders and their ideas that have impacted me before I move on to discussing food.

Student Teams

Barbara Millis conducted workshops on using groups effectively. I was interested in her material because I have been using groups for a long time but never felt that I was as effective with them as I could be.

The titles of her workshops will give an idea of her approach: "Using Groups Wisely and Well," "Promoting Deep Learning/Critical Thinking through Cooperative Activities," "Sequencing Cooperative Activities for Course Redesign," and "Cooperative Learning through Groups and Games." Note that *games* recurs in the titles, as does *cooperative*. (For more discussion, see Millis and Cottell 1998.)

As Millis has presented it, cooperative learning can be characterized as follows. First, it is "a structured form of small group problem solving that incorporates the use of heterogeneous teams." Second, it "maintains individual accountability." Third, it "promotes positive interdependence and instills group processing." Finally, it "sharpens social skills."

Millis is a proponent of using groups and prefers groups of four, a size that I now use and that I call *Teams*. As I use them, these Teams are permanent (in my case, semester-long) groups that work together in cooperative learning activities and have a division of labor in terms of what each individual is asked to do. Each Team has a permanent folder into which I put assignments and where students place the work they turn in. Team roles include a "Folder Monitor," who keeps track of the folders and has each member sign the roll; the "Facilitator," who keeps the Team on task and makes sure discussion is relevant to the class; the "Recorder," who writes down material relevant to class discussion (and is usually the person I ask to share that material with the class); and the "Reporter," who is responsible for giving oral reports on Team deliberations to the class or other Teams. Usually I try to rotate the roles periodically so that everyone gets to share. Before employng this method, I had used groups in my classes but had not been as systematic in creating and using them as Millis and others advocate.

When handled in the ways that Millis suggests, Teams can be beneficial to the course by providing a way for each member to support the others and by getting all members to participate in completing the work done. Some students complain that they dislike working in groups, that some members are slack, and that only some do the actual work. Millis offers ways to get all members to do more and to identify Team members who are and are not cooperating. For example, currently after every major Team project, I have each Team member anonymously and confidentially fill out a "Peer Evaluation" form, where each Team member gives specific information about the contributions of each member to the project. I use these forms to evaluate each member's work on the project so there is individual accountability. I also try to have a mixture of assignments done by individuals and by Teams, so I can tell where the work is being done.

I have just begun to use the practical ideas found in an article by Barbara Oakley, Rebecca Brent, Richard Felder, and Imad Elhajj, "Turning Student Groups into Effective Teams" (2004), which gives step-by-step suggestions for getting the most out of teams, including policy statements and forms useful for rating individual and team performance, among others.

Course Design

Beyond the use of cooperative groups is the issue of more systematic course structuring for student learning. I have been influenced here by a workshop by Dee Fink, who has codified his thinking into the book *Creating Significant Learning Experiences: An Integrated Approach to Designing College Courses* (2003). For Fink, what a student carries away from the course is much more than just the content. For example, his "Taxonomy of Significant Learning" (2003, 30) includes the following topics arranged in a circle so that none comes before the other:

- Foundational Knowledge
- Application
- Integration
- Human Dimension
- Caring
- Learning How to Learn

Fink is especially concerned that teachers should plan courses starting with learning objectives, what one wants students to get out of the course, and then work back to the actual assignments and day-to-day activities. The activities should be subordinate to the goals of the course. He also advocates a series of interlocked objectives that engage the student as a person and a learner, not just objectives that emphasize content.

I have used Fink's ideas in "Topics in Cultural Anthropology," the principal cultural anthropology course for the department. It is listed as a Sociology course (Sociology 300) since my department is a Department of Sociology and Social Work. In addition to being required for departmental sociology majors, the course is taken primarily by freshmen and sophomores from a wide variety of majors as their principal social science course, since it has no prerequisites. For Sociology majors, it usually constitutes their only exposure to anthropology.

Perhaps the main idea I carried away from the workshops is that actual content is one of the less important parts of a course. That doesn't mean that content is not important; it means that students don't remember much of the content unless they receive it in ways they can relate to and find interesting. I have had a difficult time wrapping my mind around this point, even though my experience tells me that it is true.

Activities that Promote Active Learning

Fink and others are also concerned with what they call "active learning," that the students are actively involved in their own education and feel empowered to make that happen for themselves. I reproduce here, with slight variations in wording and formatting, a table from Fink (2003, 108) that outlines "Activities that Promote Active Learning."

	Getting Information and Ideas	Experiencing by Doing	Experiencing by Observing	Reflecting (on what and how one is learning)
Direct Methods	Original data Original sources	Real doing, in authentic settings	Direct observation of phenomena	Classroom discussions, Term papers, In-depth reflective dialogue and writing on the learning process
Indirect, Vicarious	Secondary data and sources, Lectures, texts	Case studies, Simulations, Role playing	Stories, accessed via film, literature, oral history, etc.	
Distance Learning (online courses, interactive video, correspondence courses)	Course web site, Internet, Video lectures, Printed materials	Teacher can assign students to "directly experience..." Students can engage in indirect kinds of experience, at distant sites or online	Teacher can assign students to "directly experience..." Students can engage in indirect kinds of experience, at distant sites or online	Students can record their reflections, and then, if they choose, share their reflections with others in writing, via TV, or online

Table 1. (From Fink 2003, 108)

Fink has a lot of things he wants us to consider in designing a course. He is bringing together what he wants students to know with methods that help them relate the new knowledge to what they knew before, preferably using methods that are memorable, and that involve activities both in and outside the classroom. When I have students reflect on their learning during the semester in their Learning Portfolios, they often say that they prefer "hands-on" activities. My challenge, as I see it, is to find activities that we can do, both in and outside the classroom, that allow them to see relationships between what I am bringing to them and the activities and knowledge they have in their world outside the classroom. This is a tall challenge, but it keeps me motivated to work at making it happen, since the payoff is excitement and learning for myself and my students.

Evaluation Methods

To follow Fink's ideas about the course and about building in ways to get feedback on student learning and evaluate that learning, I created an outline of the semester's activities, including a timeline specifying what projects and activities were due at what time. For consistent feedback on student learning, I had students write a series of "Logs" that were due about every two weeks and that were designed to have students capture their thoughts and feelings about the learning process at those frequent intervals. They were asked to respond to the "Questions for the Log" that appear in Appendix 1.

At the end of the semester, students summarized these logs and the other semester activities in their Learning Portfolio. The outline of what was to be in the portfolio was given in the syllabus itself. Specific requirements for the portfolio are given in Appendix 2.

Fink suggests that it is very effective to have a major project or two that can involve a lot of the course objectives and reinforce them in memorable ways. With that in mind, and while we're digesting Fink's message, I want to move on to talk about some of these projects and how they relate to the course.

Teaching with Food

Ethnography

In terms of activities that fit with my overall course objectives and that involve active learning, I want to talk here about two—skills in interviewing and activities with food—that provide ways for comparisons and contrasts between cultural foodways. These objectives are related two objectives of the course that require both *application* and *integration* of knowledge.

For the interviewing part, I required each student to buy McCurdy, Spradley and Shandy's book *The Cultural Experience: Ethnography in Complex Society* (2005), which lays out an ethnosemantic system for doing interviews and constructing ethnographies based on them. Each team was required to choose one member of the team to do an extended ethnography on one of his or her microcultures. I tried to model the process by reviewing parts of the book and then by interviewing a volunteer class member. This particular student volunteer shared his knowledge of his music studio and music creation, and I tape-recorded the conversation and transcribed it. I shared the transcription with the class and went over *cover terms* and other ideas in reference to the transcription, as practice in doing the work. (Note that this is a much different model for interviewing and processing the interviews than those shown nightly on the news and other media. Part of my effort in using this system is to compare and contrast it with what students are used to and to give them pointers on how to interview in the ethnosemantic way.)

Teams were asked to share with me their transcriptions so I could help them with the process and then to post their completed ethnographies on a special section of Blackboard (a web-based, course-management system that the university uses). All students were asked to read each other's ethnographies, and then we had a special poster day, when each Team put posters on the wall of the classroom giving highlights of their ethnographies. All teams were given color-coded reward stickers for first, second, and third place and were asked to "vote" for the best ethnographies by putting the stickers on the posters. This process led to some lively discussions (although I don't think everyone read all the ethnographies) and to some winners. Winning teams got candy prizes and extra points on their grades.

This ethnography project was designed to help students learn a useful skill—that of structured interviewing—and also get skills they were to use in doing an ethnography of the foodways of whatever ethnic or other group they chose for their big end-of-semester project. This assignment was designed as preparation for the larger project.

In terms of evaluation of the ethnographies themselves, each Team was to evaluate each other's ethnographies using the rubric for evaluating ethnographies given in Appendix 3. I was also concerned about whether the team members were all contributing equally to the work of doing the ethnography; and in order to get feedback on that, I had each member anonymously fill out a peer-evaluation form. This form is given in Appendix 4. I specified as often as I could that I would use the results of these forms to adjust the grade (expressed as points toward the semester's total) earned by the Team itself when awarding points to each individual member. I used this peer evaluation form for all of the major reports done by teams during the semester.

Comparisons: Farm Field Trips

Another set of class activities involved field trips to two farms that provided a range of comparisons and contrasts between philosophies and practices in agriculture.

The first trip was to A&T's own farm. Founded as an 1891 Land Grant college, A&T (hence the Agricultural and Technical part of the name) has an extensive farm in terms of acreage and in terms of the activities that it undertakes, all part of the School of Agriculture (now called the School of Agriculture and Environmental Sciences). The farm cultivates and researches a variety of animals and plants. It apparently has so many visitors and tours that it has dedicated tour wagons that can be towed behind large tractors. Our guides were agricultural graduate students and staff of the Agricultural Extension Service. We were not able to see the poultry unit but got to visit the beef pens, horses, and small animals (goats and sheep). Our main focus was on the vegetable crops, which were mostly played out by the time in the fall semester when we took the tour. What interested me about the tour—which I have now done two years in a row—is that by the second year, all the crops shown to us were claimed to be "organic," since those kinds of crops were said to fetch the highest prices. (See the "Farm Assignment" in Appendix 5.)

The other trip was to the "Handance Farm," a small farm run by a husband-and-wife team who bring their produce to the Farmers Curb Market, located in a city building right down the street from campus. (A visit to this market was an optional extra-credit assignment.) The couple is practicing CSA (community shares agriculture), which involves selling shares in their upcoming harvest to interested customers. In return, the customers get bags of vegetables each week (usually during the Saturday market time) during the season. The farm is located about twenty miles north of Greensboro, and the proprietor gave us a tour of the premises, including what was left of their crops for the year, and also their own chickens and turkeys, and their recently started shiitake mushroom logs. (Incidentally, the couple is involved in the local "Slow Food" movement, but neither I nor they talked much about this social movement because of time constraints and the focus on the farm itself. This movement is certainly another source of comparisons for food studies.) (The assignment for this trip is given in Appendix 6.)

We discussed what the term "organic" means and heard the proprietors' take on its usefulness now that it is an official category sanctioned by the USDA (United States Department of Agriculture). They pointed out that they do not label their food as "organic" even though they follow organic practices, since they don't want to put up with the paperwork and costs involved in the certification process.

The visits to the two farms provided a comparison between two sets of farming practices, the small scale farm and the agribusiness-oriented university farm, and students wrote some thoughtful essays about the comparisons. One of the comparisons that came through loudest, however, was how "messy" the students thought the small farm was. Those who had family members who had gardens remarked that their families would never have anything that messy. They thought that the A&T farm looked much better, with its neat rows and delineated crop areas.

Comparisons: Meals

I also had students do an assignment where they described and analyzed a major meal that they witnessed or partook of, using an analysis scheme I developed with Sandrea Williamson, a history department colleague with whom I have collaborated for many years on assignments and field trips. (See "Meal Context Analysis Checklist" in Appendix 7.)

As an in-class practice for this, I dusted off a set of films that I have used for years in various classes, *Four Families* (1959), with Margaret Mead and Ian McNeill of the Canadian Broadcasting System. Although designed to showcase ideas about infant enculturation, each vignette (about fifteen minutes each) from four cultures

(India, France, Japan, Canada) features a complete meal with the entire family as part of the video. This meal component allows for analysis of social, cultural, and technological factors involved in the meal (through using the Meal Context Analysis Checklist). It also invites comparisons and contrasts among the cultures and with what the students observe in their own family or in another context that they studied. (They were especially encouraged to do a homecoming meal or Thanksgiving meal.)

Comparisons: Foodways

An ongoing major project during the semester was the study of the book *Everyone Eats: Understanding Food and Culture,* by E. N. Anderson (2005). Each Team was responsible for giving a brief review of a chapter to the class, with comparisons to the *Four Family* film and other materials. The dates for these reports were in the "Weekly Steps" outline given at the beginning of the semester. (The rubric for evaluating these reports is given in Appendix 8 as "Criteria for Evaluating Team Reports on Book Chapters.")

While this review was going on, each Team was charged with finding an informant and researching his or her foodways and with doing an ethnosemantic ethnography called the "Global Meal Report." The criteria can be seen by referring to Appendix 7. The assignment was described in an information sheet, "Expectations for Global Meal Project" (Appendix 9).

The charge to the Teams was to: (a) find a local informant, (b) do an ethnography of his or her foodways, leading up to (c) getting a recipe from them, and (d) providing samples of the food cooked from that recipe to be presented to the class as part of a ten-minute, oral report on the ethnographies.

This charge led to some lively reports, including several where the informants did most of the presentation. The students reported on

Kenyan food, West Indian food, some Asian varieties. The presentations included one by a local gentleman who is an advocate of raw foods and who handed out cards advertising his business.

In terms of evaluation, a couple of assignments are related to this project; one is the "Global Meal Expectations" assignment, and the other is the "Criteria for Evaluating Team Reports on Global Meal," used to evaluate the project (Appendix 10).

Unfortunately, for the semester I am reporting on, this project got started late enough in the semester that the ethnographies were not particularly comprehensive. Most of the reports were given on the last two days of class, with the result that a lot of food was eaten but the reports were hurried. (With this project, there seemed to be a lot of the different foods being eaten by class members, although by no means did all members taste all the food. This was in contrast with a previous incarnation of this course, which I have done in collaboration with Ms. Williamson, where the students brought in foods cooked with recipes, ingredients, and technologies as they would have been prepared in 1859. In many cases with these foods, the students would bring their assigned nineteenth-century food but refuse to eat any of it.)

For review of what I have been covering, we can consider how the activities and assignments fit into Fink's model. Direct methods included Spradley-style interviews, field trips, the global meal research and reports, logs, and learning portfolios. Indirect methods included lectures and texts, video, and the Blackboard system class website. I used materials from the various projects reviewed above, exams, and the end of the semester Learning Portfolio, to assess how close the course came to fulfilling the objectives given earlier in this paper. Based on my assessment criteria, I conclude that overall the students met the goals I outlined for the semester, including gaining knowledge of food and foodways, the ability to do interviews and analysis, and the ability to do comparisons between cultural systems. The course was a success on those scores.

Conclusion—"Carry Out" Lessons

I have two of what I call "carry out" (in reference to the food theme) conclusions I want to share here. One is that the group process with the teams takes a lot of time, especially class time, and I need to provide more time for it but structure it so that it is productive. For this course, I had so many projects that we didn't do them justice. The other conclusion is to find ways to model or show what the result of an assignment should be so that students will know what to strive for. I cannot assume that students will know what I want from an assignment (such as an analysis of a meal) unless I can model it or give a cogent example. I did that to some extent with the Ethnography project but not enough with the others; as a consequence I don't think the students knew what they were to produce. I have been using Rubrics for assessment, but did not take the time to go over those and to model outcomes. [See my comments on "Scaffolding" in the postscript below.]

A Recommended Treat

I do not claim to have command of the literature on foods and foodways but want to recommend an author whose books have helped me think about food. Michael Pollan's work appears in the *New York Times* as well as in books. One of his latest books, which parallels some of what anthropologists talk about in terms of subsistence patterns, is *The Omnivore's Dilemma: A Natural History of Four Meals* (2006). At the time I was preparing this paper, he also published a valuable article in the *New York Times* that seems to summarize a lot of his thinking. It is called "Unhappy Meals," and was printed in the January 28, 2007, issue. A later book, *In Defense of Food* (2008), seems to be an expansion of this article.

Postscript (or should it be labeled "Dessert?")
Continuing in the tradition of "chef's surprise," I want to add some comments stemming from a recent workshop held by Craig Nelson, a long-time thinker in the area of the scholarship of teaching and learning. As I understand his story, his involvement in this area came from his studying ways to decrease the number of students who did poorly, or failed courses in his area—that of biology. He cites the work of Treisman (1986), who discovered that changing one's pedagogy can make a dramatic difference in the outcomes of students studying in mathematics. Here, I want to highlight some ideas I got from Nelson (1994) and the workshop he conducted at my institution.

The first idea is that of *mental models*—both those that the students bring with them to college and to any of our courses—and also those of the disciplines they study. The fact that students' brains are not tabulae rasae when they reach us should be obvious to anthropologists who are using the concept of culture to understand the world of human behavior. Nelson shows that it is important for faculty to find ways to explore what these student models are and build from these to what they want students to learn. Nelson suggests ways for students to do out-of-class exercises that are then shared with small groups of students in class so that all involved can make explicit what they bring with them and study it in light of what the instructor brings. In this way, Nelson advocates the use of small groups of students who are teaching and learning from each other, which ties in with what I have said above about Barbara Millis's work.

The other kind of mental model is that of the discipline that is being studied, which often has methods and expectations, as well as definitions of key terms that are different from what students probably learned before they entered the profession, and often different from what other disciplines they may be studying at the same time are doing or expecting. An example here is the concept of *culture*; anthropologists have argued for generations about what it is and have struggled for the definitive definition (or definitions?) of this key concept. But our use of the term is different from what students may meet in English or literature courses, and certainly different from what they meet in biology. Students need for us as instructors to make these differences explicit and to reinforce their learning about them.

Tied into these models are many unspoken approaches and concepts that can trip up students. Many of us, as well-socialized members of the profession, have so internalized these concepts that we forget about them and are puzzled when students cannot use them on assignments. For example, there are widely varying standards of proof and steps to defining problems between disciplines, and these differences can be dizzying for students. In literary studies, one may prove a thesis by relating it to other parts of the text that is being studied without any use made of empirical data. This approach is sometimes used in parts of anthropology, while other types of anthropology require certain kinds of field research to be conducted in order to find the information that can be used to prove a thesis, often with certain kinds of statistics displayed as evidence of proof. In many cases, these differences in approaches and proof are not explicitly taught by the instructors, who expect students to infer this from examples or from study of professional literature. This lack of explicitness brings me to the second point, which is sometimes referred to by Nelson and others as *scaffolding*.

Scaffolding refers to a process by which an instructor gives students, in a series of assignments and exercises, the skills and experience needed for them to conduct the kinds of assignments and to perform proofs that are in line with what is demanded by the discipline being studied. I tried to do this with my course by having us all study the McCurdy book and do a "practice" ethnography of a member of the Team before tackling the "real" ethnography of a food item for the final project. As part of the practice, we were all supposed to read one or more of the student ethnographies that are part of the Spradley book. I did not spend class time in the study of any particular one of those, since I *assumed* that students would get the connection between the ethnography in the book and the steps to creating their own that we were reviewing in class. I think my assumption was incorrect; when I do this again, I will assign a particular one of the ethnographies, and then have the teams review each member's understandings of it, and provide a way for the whole class to do a review before we move on to the step of creating our own ethnographies.

For me, learning of the achievements that have been made by applying Nelson's ideas for improving teaching and learning is inspirational. Of course, it sounds easy when the masters discuss them, but applying them to one's own work and teaching requires constant work. I hope that this article has given my readers some ideas and inspiration to do this sort of work themselves.

Works Cited

Anderson, E. N. 2005. *Everyone Eats: Understanding Food and Culture*. New York: New York University Press.

Fink, D. 2003. *Creating Significant Learning Experiences: An Integrated Approach to Designing College Courses*. San Francisco: Jossey-Bass.

Four Families (film). 1959. New York: National Film Board of Canada.

McCurdy, D., James P. Spradley, and Dianna J. Shandy. 2005. *The Cultural Experience: Ethnography in Complex Society*, 2nd ed. Long Grove, IL: Waveland Press.

Millis, B. J., and P. G. Cottell. 1998. *Cooperative Learning for Higher Education Faculty*. Phoenix: Oryx Press.

Nelson, C. E. 1994. "Critical Thinking and Collaborative Learning." *New Directions for Teaching and Learning* 59:45-58.

Oakley, B., Rebecca Brent, Richard M. Felder, and Imad Elhajj. 2004. "Turning Student Groups into Effective Teams." *Journal of Student Centered Learning* 2:9-34.

Pollan, M. 2006. *The Ominvore's Dilemma: A Natural History of Four Meals*. New York: Penguin.

———. 2007. "Unhappy Meals." *New York Times*, January 28.

———. 2008. *In Defense of Food*. New York: Penguin.

Treisman, U. 1986. "A Study of the Mathematics Performance of Black Students at the University of California, Berkeley." PhD diss. University of California, Berkeley. Dissertation Abstracts International (47: 1641A).

Appendix 1

Questions for the Log

(The following are suggested questions to write about briefly to gather material for your logs, which will be part of the material for your Learning Portfolio.)

At what moment <u>in class</u> this week (or in the past couple of weeks) were you most engaged as a learner? What do you think contributed to this engagement?

At what moment <u>in class</u> this week (or in the past couple of weeks) were you most distanced as a learner? What contributed to this disengagement?

At what moment during your <u>out of class</u> work this week (or in the past couple of weeks) were you most engaged as a learner? What do you think contributed to this engagement?

At what moment during your <u>out of class</u> work this week (or in the past couple of weeks) were you most distanced as a learner? What contributed to this disengagement?

What action taken by anyone in the room took during class this week did you find the most affirming or positive or helpful?

What action taken by anyone in the room took during the class this week did you find the most puzzling or confusing?

What surprised you most about the class this week or in the past couple of weeks?

What have you learned about your learning styles and abilities during the past couple of weeks? How are you going to use this knowledge to help you learn better?

For stat class: What have you learned about your learning when you compare your performance on the quizzes with the Team performance?

What resources do you think you need in order to learn better? How are you going to get these resources?

Appendix 2

Learning Portfolio

This is a notebook created by each student that contains his or her work during the semester, logs of experiences, and reflections on learning. The rubric that the instructor will use to mark the portfolio will be shared with the class during the semester.

The portfolio will have an extended essay, with supporting exhibits of work, that discusses the following:

> a. What *key ideas or information* have you learned about the subject of this course?
>
> b. What have you learned about *how to use or apply* the content of the course?
>
> c. What parts of your knowledge, thinking, or actions have you been able to *integrate* or connect within or external to this learning experience? In other words, what knowledge or thinking or behaviors have you been able to relate to other parts within the course and to other parts of your life outside the course?
>
> d. What have you learned about the *human dimension* of the subject? That is, how have you changed in some important way, and how have you changed in your ability to interact with *others*?
>
> e. What interests, feelings, or *values* have changed as a result of this learning experience?
>
> f. What have you learned about *how to learn*?

Appendix 3

Team # _____

Marking Rubric for evaluating the Ethnographies
(taken from Spradley, Chapter 9)

1. Thesis statement: concise statement of what the ethnography is about

                        2   4   6

2. Parts of the paper

    Lead section (clarity, detail)

                        5   10   15

    Methods used in the data gathering

                        2   4   6

    Methods used in protecting informants (use of pseudonyms, masking people, places, events) 2   4   6

    Cultural Setting for the ethnography

                        2   4   6   8

    Body of paper

        Use of analytical taxonomies   5   10   15

        Narrative discussion   5   10   15

    Conclusion   5   10

    Total   _____

    Bonus from Class   + _____

Total Points for Team _____

Comments:

Note: Individual Team member's scores may be different based on evaluations by other Team members.

Member Scores:

_____   _____
_____   _____
_____   _____
_____   _____

Appendix 4

Peer Evaluation of Team Member's Contributions to the Oral Report (to be filled out anonymously and returned to the instructor)

Class _____ Team # _____ Title of Report _____

Column One

Name of Team Member

Column Two

Specific contributions made to the creation of the ethnography

Column Three

Points earned (0-10 scale) with 10 highest

Appendix 5

Assignment for Field Trip to A&T Farm (Greensboro, NC)

Purpose: The purpose of the trip is to learn about the operation of the A&T farm itself and to learn about agricultural practices that the operators of the farm demonstrate and advocate.

Directions to Site: (Specifics are given)

Assignment: The workshop will be led by . . . and . . . members of the local Ag Extension program.

Listen to what the leaders have to say and record information about how the farm is laid out, what kinds of things it does, and especially what you can learn about the agricultural products and processes that it teaches about and is researching.

Written Assignment: Do a write-up about the trip in which you briefly discuss:
      a) what you learned about the farm
      b) the two ideas/artifacts/experiences you found the most interesting about the trip
      c) how the trip compares/contrasts with Handance trip
      d) two terms/concepts from the Anderson book

Due date and value for written assignment:
Typed or computer-written assignment is due within 1½ weeks from time of trip; value is 100 points. This assignment is to be done by INDIVIDUALS!

Appendix 6

Assignment for Field Trip to Handance Farm (near Reidsville, NC)
Travel date: XXXXX

Purpose: The purpose of the trip is to learn about the operation of the farm itself and to learn about organic, agricultural practices that the operators of the farm demonstrate and advocate.

Directions to Site: (Specifics are given)

NOTE: The trip will involve walking around the site, so wear comfortable walking shoes and suitable coats, sweaters, etc. depending on the weather.

Assignment: The workshop will be led by the farm owners/operators.
    1. Listen to what they have to say about the farm and the kinds of crops/animals they raise and also to their discussion of organic farming methods, as well as their CSA initiative.
    2. Record information about how the farm is laid out, what kinds of things it does, and especially what you can learn about organic agricultural products and processes.

Written Assignment: Do a write-up about the trip in which you include:
    a) your map of how the farm is laid out and what crops and animals, etc. are where,
    b) a brief discussion of what you learned about the farm and how it is operated,

c) a comparison and contrast of what you learned at this farm and A&T's farm, and

d) a brief discussion of two ideas/artifacts/experiences you found most interesting about the trip.

Due date and value for written assignment:

Typed or computer-written assignment is due within 1½ weeks from time of trip; value is 100 points. This assignment is to be done by INDIVIDUALS!

Appendix 7

Meal Context Analysis Checklist
by David Johnson and Sandrea Williamson

1. Social context:
    - What is the name of meal (if it has a name)?
    - Who is present (status and economic condition of people being served and eating and of those doing the serving)?
    - How do they sit? What kinds of clothing do they wear?
    - What do they sit at (table, floor, etc.)?
    - Who is in charge, if anyone?
    - What kinds of topics are discussed?
    - Who cooks; who serves; who is served (in terms of age/gender or other statuses); in what order?
    - When does the meal start? When does it stop?
    - Who decides when it will start and stop?
    - When is it held; is it considered an ordinary, everyday meal, or a special ritual meal (such as a holiday, religious, or political occasion) or some special occasion?
    - Who is in charge of cleaning up and who is expected to help with the clean up and resetting of the area to a non-meal status (gender/age/ethnicity/other status)?

2. Foods and preparation
Food items presented at the meal:
    - What foods were used for the meal? For each, discuss the source of the food (who grew it, when and how).
    - What status/economic factors were involved in food choices (such as costs for sugar or meats or other items)

- What kinds of preparation procedures are used (such as baking, frying, serving raw) and what preparations go with what foods?
- What kinds of technological devices are needed to process them?
(and see below)
- What work process is used to prepare the foods?
- What kinds of foods are presented to the assembled group?
- What is the order of presentation of the food? List any foods that are considered defining of that kind of meal (such as turkey at Thanksgiving, etc.).
- What foods would not be considered appropriate (such as hot dogs for breakfast for many Americans)?
- Who is expected to prepare the foods (gender/age/ethnicity/other status)?
- Who is expected to serve the foods (gender/age/ethnicity/other status), if not the preparer?

3. Technology

　1) Food preparation
　What items are used to create the meal in the cooking area? For each item, discuss:

- Who made these? When are they considered routine and ordinary, or special?
- Were they created by the owners or users or bought from some outside source?
- Who are the owners of the items?
- Are the items expensive or ordinary?
- Are they part of the fixed furniture of the kitchen or cook area (such as stoves) or movable?
- Where are they stored?

Describe where the meal is prepared (for example, in a special room, in a building outside of the main house, or elsewhere).

2) Food serving
- What kinds of items are used to serve and to consume the foods?
- What items go with what kinds of foods?
- Where are these stored when not in use?

3) Food consumption area
- Describe the area where the food is consumed and the kinds of fixed and movable objects used for such consumption.
- Describe how this area is related to other parts of the dwelling.

4) Summary
- Why is this information important?
- What have we learned about gender roles and individual or group statuses?

Appendix 8

Criteria for Evaluating Team Reports on Book Chapters

Presenters' Team # _____ and Title of Chapter _____

Team # of Evaluator _____ (Note: Evaluator should come to class having read the chapter and Team online report)

I. Online Summary of Chapter
- displays knowledge of chapter material
- uses clear and understandable visual aids
- uses correct spelling and grammar
- shows main points of chapter
- coincides well with class component of report
- submitted on time

Max Value: 25 points

Value assigned by evaluator: _____

Comments on evaluation:

II. In Class Presentation of Chapter
- shows knowledge of subject; includes ability to answer questions from class members
- wears appropriate dress
- uses good communication skills; includes body language
- includes a contribution from every member of the Team
- gets the class involved
- provides an outline with comments tying to class activities
- shows creativity and enthusiasm
- demonstrates timeliness and preparedness by all members
- uses an appropriate length

Max Value: 25 points
Value assigned by evaluator: _____
Comments on evaluation:

Total points earned by Team _____

Appendix 9

Expectations for Global Meal Project

The Global Meal Project will involve each Team's locating an informant who has a foodway different from the majority of those in the Team. This can be someone from a different ethnic background but can also include someone from a different generation or subculture (such as, for example, a vegetarian, meat eater, unprocessed food eater) who is willing to share his or her knowledge with the Team. The informant can include a member of the Team who is willing to share with the rest of the class; if the Team wishes to use a Team member as an informant, it needs to clear this with Dr. Johnson.

The Team will do an ethnographic study of the person's foodways, with the focus on a particular recipe that the Team, or the Team in conjunction with the informant, will cook and present to the class as a whole.

On the day agreed upon by the class, the Team will present the food, along with a brief oral report about the summary of their ethnography to the class, and the Team will have their complete ethnography available on Blackboard.

The class will judge the presentation using a form similar to the one used for chapter and Contemporary Issues projects. The maximum value for the meal will be 150 points.

Appendix 10

Criteria for Evaluating Team Reports on Global Meal

Presenters' Team # _____ and Title of Report _____
(Note: Presenter Team will fill out Peer Evaluation form on each member's contributions.)

Team # of Evaluator _____

Characteristics of the Team and its presentation (maximum 45 percent)

- shows knowledge of subject   5   10
  (includes ability to answer questions from class members)
- appropriate dress   5
- uses good communication skills   10
  (includes body language)
- every member makes a contribution 5
- report gets class involved   5
- creative and enthusiastic   5
- all members are on time and prepared 5

Characteristics of the material presented (maximum 55 percent)

- team gives clear outline of what the presentation will cover   5
- presentation is an appropriate length   5   10
- thorough coverage of topic   10   15   20   25   30
- shows adequate research   5   10

Comments on evaluation:

What was done well?

Contributors*

AVI BRISMAN is an assistant professor at the School of Justice Studies, College of Justice and Safety, Eastern Kentucky University.

DAVID COZZO is an ethnobotanist and Area Specialized Agent for the North Carolina Cooperative Extension based at the Eastern Band of the Cherokee Indians Extension Center and is the Project Director for the Revitalization of Traditional Cherokee Artisan Resources.

C. LAINE GATES, at the time this paper was presented, was a graduate student in the Department of Anthropology, University of Arkansas.

DAVID M. JOHNSON is an associate professor in the Sociology and Social Work Department at North Carolina A&T State University in Greensboro, North Carolina.

LISA J. LEFLER is a medical anthropologist and the Director of Culturally Based Native Health Programs at Western Carolina University. She is also founder and Executive Director of the Center for Native Health, Inc.

JUSTIN M. NOLAN is an associate professor and Vice-Chair of the Department of Anthropology, University of Arkansas.

Mary Jo Schneider is Professor Emerita in the Department of Anthropology, University of Arkansas.

---

* Note: This information reflects affiliations that were current in 2012 and does not reflect changes since then.

www.ingramcontent.com/pod-product-compliance
Lightning Source LLC
Chambersburg PA
CBHW032255150426
43195CB00008BA/466